HEGEMONY

KEY IDEAS
Series Editor: Peter Hamilton
The Open University

KEY IDEAS

Series Editor: PETER HAMILTON
The Open University, Milton Keynes

Designed to complement the successful *Key Sociologists*, this series covers the main concepts, issues, debates, and controversies in sociology and the social sciences. The series aims to provide authoritative essays on central topics of social science, such as community, power, work, sexuality, inequality, beliefs and ideology, class, family, etc. Books adopt a strong individual 'line' constituting original essays rather than literary surveys, and form lively and original treatments of their subject matter. The books will be useful to students and teachers of sociology, political science, economics, psychology, philosophy, and geography.

THE SYMBOLIC CONSTRUCTION OF COMMUNITY
ANTHONY P. COHEN, Department of Social Anthropology, University of Manchester

SOCIETY
DAVID FRISBY and DEREK SAYER, Department of Sociology, University of Glasgow

SEXUALITY
JEFFREY WEEKS, Social Work Studies Department, University of Southampton

WORKING
GRAEME SALAMAN, Faculty of Social Sciences, The Open University, Milton Keynes

BELIEFS AND IDEOLOGY
KENNETH THOMPSON, Faculty of Social Sciences, The Open University, Milton Keynes

EQUALITY
BRYAN TURNER, School of Social Sciences, The Flinders University of South Australia

HEGEMONY
ROBERT BOCOCK, Faculty of Social Sciences, The Open University, Milton Keynes

HEGEMONY

ROBERT BOCOCK
Faculty of Social Sciences
The Open University, Milton Keynes

ELLIS HORWOOD LIMITED
Publishers · Chichester

TAVISTOCK PUBLICATIONS
London and New York

First published in 1986 by
ELLIS HORWOOD LIMITED
Market Cross House, Cooper Street,
Chichester, Sussex, PO19 1EB, England
and
TAVISTOCK PUBLICATIONS LIMITED
11 New Fetter Lane, London EC4P 4EE

Published in the USA by
TAVISTOCK PUBLICATIONS
and ELLIS HORWOOD LIMITED
in association with METHUEN INC.
29 West 35th Street, New York, NY 10001–2291

British Library Cataloguing in Publication Data
Bocock, Robert
Hegemony. — (Key ideas)
1. Social classes   2. Ideology
I. Title   II. Series
305.5   HT609
Library of Congress CIP Data also available

ISBN 0–7458–0107–2 (Ellis Horwood Limited — Library Edn.)
ISBN 0–7458–0118–8 (Ellis Horwood Limited — Student Edn.)

Phototypeset in Times by Ellis Horwood Limited
Printed in Great Britain by R.J. Acford, Chichester

Contents

Robert James Bocock is Senior Lecturer in Sociology at the Open University, Milton Keynes, a position he has held since 1979. He was formerly Lecturer in Sociology at Brunel University, London (1966–79), and has, since 1968, additionally lectured in sociology at The Richmond Fellowship College in London. He has a Ph.D. in Sociology and a B.A. in Sociology and Philosophy .

Dr. Bocock is the author of several articles for the *British Journal of Sociology,* editor of *An Introduction to Sociology* (1980), co-editor with K. Thompson, *Religion and Ideology* (1985), and author of *Ritual in Industrial Society* (1974), *Freud and Modern Society* (1976) and *Sigmund Freud* (1983). He has researched and lectured in the USA, Canada, and Tanzania.

Editor's foreword

The key ideas around which debate and controversy revolve are constantly in a state of flux. This is nowhere more obvious than in the social sciences, where the conceptual and methodological debates which animate the disciplines are intimately (although not always obviously) linked to crises and changes in the social world beyond the University's real or symbolic walls.

Thus it is that a concept developed by an obscure Italian Marxist — Gramsci — has come to stand for both the intellectual polyversity of modern social thought, and one of Marxism's most serious conceptual problems.

At base, hegemony is all about ideology. But it is ideology writ large: the idea of an all-encompassing dominant ideology whose scope extends throughout all social, cultural and economic spheres of a society. Some German social thinkers in the late nineteenth and early twentieth centuries talked about world-views or *weltanschauungen* — a term they had taken over from art history and literary studies to describe what Gramsci was attempting to put in an authentically Marxist form. Hegemony is the concept a Marxist would use to describe a world-view whose effect is to congeal the dominance of one economic class over another into cultural permanence.

Gramsci was of course the archetypal victim of the condition he was diagnosing. Like many a sociologist his understanding of the underpinnings of his society was formed through a marginalizing experience. His was of a rather extreme variety, being thrown into prison during that period of confusion and repression which followed Mussolini's accession to power in the mid-1920s, and only being released shortly before his death.

Gramsci's ideas were formed by his experience of political action prior to imprisonment, and crystallized during his lengthy incarceration. His concept of hegemony was thus a product of a social context quite different to that of the present day in most of Europe and North America. How, then, has it come to provide the focus for contemporary debate about culture and society?

In linking the Marxist problematic of social change to the historical observation that no Western society has experienced a successful proletarian revolution, Robert Bocock shows why Gramsci's ideas exercise such influence today.

If the working class in the West has lost its desire for fundamental social change — even during the worst economic recession since the 1930s — does the explanation lie in ideological or 'cultural' factors?

Gramsci faced a similar problem in Italy — the failure of the Italian working class to mount a revolution against the fascist state and its bourgeois supporters. His conclusions centred on the interdependence of the economic, political and cultural spheres and their domination by 'elites' which shared a fundamental world-view or 'hegemonic' outlook.

Those social thinkers who today use Gramsci's ideas — and they include a wide range of influential writers, from Stuart Hall to Anthony Giddens — are preoccupied with a problematic which would be recognizable to Gramsci. It is the utter dominance of capitalism as a social system in Western society, despite (and almost, it seems, because of) its failure to solve underlying problems of political, economic and social inequality.

That this dominance is 'hegemonic' to use Gramsci's terminology derives primarily from the perception of the majority of society that the present structure of the social system is legitimate, to a greater or lesser extent. It is important to recognize, as Dr Bocock points out, that Gramsci's use of the concept of hegemony is firmly differentiated both from the Marxist notion of ideology on the one hand and Max Weber's use of the concept of legitimacy on the other. It is the sheer taken-for-grantedness of hegemony that yields its full effects — the 'naturalness' of a way of thinking about social, economic, political and ethical issues. This makes the theory of hegemony much richer or more encompassing than the restricted concepts of ideology and legitimacy, which are used to define either distorted conceptions of reality or methods of inducing consent and acquiescence in a political system.

As Robert Bocock shows so effectively in this indispensable introduction to Gramsci's influence on modern social thought, the study of hegemonic processes invites a *rapprochement* of philosophy and social science. It is in this area that the application of Gramsci's ideas has so much to say to contemporary social theory. Swayed as it is by the winds of competing theoretical perspectives, modern sociology has tended to ignore philosophical approaches to many of the issues with which it grapples. As this book so helpfully shows, the concept of hegemony is both a way of understanding the world-view of contemporary capitalism, and a way of returning its critique to more fundamental philosophical questions.

Peter Hamilton

Preface

My interest in the idea of hegemony has developed both from working on the Open University course 'Beliefs and Ideologies' and from my research in the sociology of religion and on Freudian social theory.

The research and writing I have done over the last fifteen years has involved work on ritual action in modern Britain which led me to take an interest in psychoanalytic approaches to ritual action in political, life-cycle, aesthetic and religious contexts. My interests also developed in the implications of psychoanalysis for the sociology of morals. This in turn linked back to my interest in the sociology of religion more generally. It is in this context that I have recently turned to an examination of the concept of hegemony. This is part of a wider concern with which world-view, if any, whether religious or political, operates to underpin moral values about politics, economics, military matters and sexuality in modern Britain and other Western societies.

Many people, both in work situations and outside them, have played a part in the discussions which have helped me to develop this work on hegemony. These include the members of the Open University course team on 'Beliefs and Ideologies' — Veronica Beechey, James Donald, Stuart Hall, Gregor McLennan and Kenneth Thompson particularly. I would also like to acknowledge the staff and students at the Richmond Fellowship College in London who have helped stimulate my research and writing in the period during which this book has developed. The help and stimulus provided by Peter Hamilton, the series editor, has been invaluable. I have also had valuable discussions about themes relevant to this book with Jean Bocock, Michael Bowman and June and John Huntington in particular. No-one mentioned above is responsible for the errors or mistaken interpretations in the book — the responsibility for these lies with the author.

Introduction

The concept of hegemony forms a central part of a wider problematic which marks a new departure in social theory for the contemporary period, even though the idea has its roots in the nineteen-twenties and -thirties. Stated briefly, it can be said at this stage that hegemony means 'moral and philosophical leadership', leadership which is attained through the active consent of major groups in a society.

As will be discussed in later chapters the concept of hegemony represents a break with economistic versions of Marxism in which emphasis is put on economic factors as the major motor of change. It also marks a break with those forms of deterministic and mechanistic Marxism in which change is seen as unproblematically brought about by the laws of history working independently of political movements and human will.

New developments in social theory such as this do not take place in a political vacuum, but against the background of events in a particular period in specific societies. This was true during the development of modern sociology in the work of Marx, Weber and Durkheim, for example, and has remained so in more recent contributions. In the case of the renewed interest in the concept of hegemony among Western European social theorists, the background influences can be seen to lie in the changing political situations in the major Western European countries. These have taken different forms in each particular country. Nevertheless there have been some common features such as the continuing growth of the European Economic Community, the relations between Western Europe and the communist regimes in the East, and the problems surrounding the role of the United States in Western European economic, military and cultural affairs.

In Britain, more specifically, the development of 'Thatcherism' from 1979 through to the time of writing in 1986 has been of paramount importance in affecting the political agenda in the society. Such a new type of right-wing political economy as that of Thatcherism has had parallels in the United States under Reagan, in West Germany, in Japan and, after the 1986 elections, in France too. The term 'monetarism' has been used sometimes to denote all these specific types of new ideology and political economy; a more general term, which includes the non-economic aspects of this phenomenon, such as the importance given to the family and sexual morality, is the phrase the 'New Right'.

This political phenomenon has exerted an influence on the concerns of sociologists and social theorists as well as on those of politicians. In Britain, for example, the nature and depths of the apparent shift of large sections of public opinion towards the acceptance of the privatization of publicly owned industries and services, and towards greater legal controls over trades unions, which has been seen from 1979 onwards, has raised serious questions about the lack of widespread acceptance of some forms of public ownership and about the role of trades unions. Trades unions have appeared to be representing the narrow economic interests of particular occupational groups, such as the miners in the 1984–85 coal strike, rather than as leading a political campaign against the new form of economic liberalism as represented by Thatcherism.

In the development of this kind of public perception the media may play some part in the constructions they give to events such as strikes; but there are wider issues involved. Most importantly it is widespread philosophical and moral ideas which influence people's perceptions. These underlying ideas and values come from religious groups, from the law, from educational institutions, from political movements and parties, more than they do from newspapers, radio or television news broadcasts. The latter deal with day-to-day events rather than with the formation of underlying philosophy and moral values. There are important sources of moral and philosophical ideas in the magazines and newspapers of religious and political groups, as well as from radio and television programmes about current affairs and religion, but it is often membership of organizations, including work organizations, which develops an interest in people to read, listen to and view these media.

It is these wider processes in a society which are addressed by the concept and problematic of hegemony. Such a concept has been thought useful by some social theorists in order to pose questions about how moral and philosophical leadership is produced in a social formation. It has led also to discussions about the extent to which a new moral and philosophical hegemony can be built up among all of the major progressive, radical, groups in Western Europe, or even in the United States. This new form of alliance could aim to include manual workers, the Women's Movement, gay people's organizations, the Peace Movement, religious groups, environmentalists, members of all ethnic groups in a society as well as people involved in occupations other than traditional manual ones. This new alliance would include workers such as engineers, nurses, doctors, teachers, journalists and those working in the broadcasting media, as well as the manual workers' trades unions and political groups. Such an alliance would form a basis for developing a new hegemonic outlook, one based upon radical philosophical and moral ideas. It would aim to be more catholic in the groups which it embraced than most existing political groups on the left.

New forms of social theory have been needed, however, over a longer time period than just the last decade, the decade during which the New Right has achieved political power and influence. There has been a need felt by some social theorists and sociologists to replace earlier dogmatic, economistic versions of Marxism in order to try to understand a social and political landscape which has changed from that found in the capitalism of the late nineteenth century or in the first half of the twentieth centruy. Some of the main debates involved in this process of the emergence of new social theory around the concept of hegemony will be sketched in this Introduction, albeit in a very condensed way. Some such background is needed for those readers who may not have been following all the twists and turns in social theory over the last few decades.

Traditional forms of Marxism have held that change would come about in advanced capitalist societies, such as those in Western Europe, as a result of the revolutionary actions of the industrial working class. There have been important debates among sociologists and social theorists about the role of the working class as a major agent of change in advanced industrial capitalist societies in Western Europe, some arguing that it is still the major potential change agent, but most holding that it is better to see the industrial working class as not only shrinking numerically but as more bound into consumer capitalism than ever before. Consequently it is argued that is necessary to look elsewhere for agents of change and for new conceptions of social change itself. This has led in turn to a debate about the political importance, or otherwise, of new types of social movement such as the Women's Movement, the Gay Movement, the Peace Movement, the Greens and other environmentalist movements, together with ethnic and national movements. These new movements have developed over the last twenty years or more largely outside the conventional political system of parties and pressure groups. They have developed new forms of social change achieved through consciousness-raising groups among women and self-help groups among gay men for instance.

An assessment of the role of the new 'middle classes' engaged in modern industrial processes, and in the large public service sector, in relationship to social-political change has also been important in the development of interest in the concept of hegemony. The dogmatic Marxist position attached sole importance to the traditional industrial working class, to educating trade unionists in that class about their political importance and potential, and to awaiting the day when a revolution would overthrow the capitalist class and abolish their ownership of the means of production, distribution and exchange. Many sociologists, among others, have cast doubt on the accuracy and plausibility of this model of modern capitalist society and have emphasized the growth of new kinds of occupations in advanced industrial capitalism. The likelihood of the industrial working class overthrowing capitalism has come to seem very questionable, to say the least, in the eyes of many social scientists and politicians committed to seeking fundamental changes in modern capitalism. It is in this political context that the recent interest in the concept of hegemony has developed for it has been hoped that such a concept, and the wider political position of which it is the central component, might offer some way of developing a new and coherent type of radical politics.

These debates have taken place in the context of the aftermath of the failure of the 1968 Spring events in France to produce a fundamental change of the French system, and of the failure of more politically conventional attempts to change modern capitalism in other Western European societies. These failures led to a major re-think of their political position on the part of those desiring more far-reching changes. The work of the French philosopher Louis Althusser became influential after 1968. This occurred as a consequence of the failure of the humanistic, existentialist perspective, which had been the dominant philosophical outlook of many of those participating in the 1968 events, to achieve lasting change of 'the system'.

Much of radical social theory came under the influence of Althusserian Marxism, both in France and elsewhere, largely as a consequence of the failure of the humanistic and critical theoretical outlook to bring about the desired changes of the system during the nineteen-sixties. The Althusserian problematic came to displace the more humanistic and Hegelian perspectives of Sartre's existentialism and of the later Frankfurt School's critical theory, such as that developed by Herbert Marcuse. These less mechanistic forms of Marxism had been influenced by the earlier pioneering work of the Hungarian social philosopher Georg Lukacs, published in his book, *History and Class Consciousness*, which was written between 1919 and 1922. It was this set of tendencies towards Hegelian, or humanistic, Marxism, which Althusser aimed to criticize.

The work of Althusser had, as one of its central aims, the elimination of 'humanism' and its associated Hegelian philosophical concepts within Marxism. Althusser claimed that Marx had produced the science of modes of production, of capitalism in particular. This development made by Marx had constituted an epistemological break with all earlier forms of humanism in philosophy and with Hegelian philosophy in particular in Althusser's view. The emphasis upon the 'scientificity' of Marxism was in direct contrast to the more philosophical, existentialist and critical theoretical, forms of Marxism found in Western Marxism before Althusser's intervention. In these forms of Marxism the emphasis has been upon the humanism in Marx's early works and upon themes such as those of alienation, estrangement, dialectical reason and praxis — all Hegelian terms to be eschewed by scientific Marxists in Althusser's view.

More recently Althusserianism has come in for criticism itself, not only in France but in Britain, Spain and Italy too. Some of the most significant of these criticisms have drawn upon the concept of hegemony. The resurgence of theoretical interest in the concept of hegemony, especially as this was developed in the work of Antonio Gramsci (1891–1937), have arisen in the context of the debate about Althusser's intervention in Marxist theory and philosophy.

However, Gramsci's notion of hegemony was located within his own humanistic reading of Marx and Marxism. In spite of this, many of the recent influential criticisms of Althusserianism have shared Althusser's 'anti-humanism', even when drawing upon Gramsci's work. Anti-humanism, as the term is used here, means fundamentally that human consciousness and subjectivity is seen as being constituted by forces outside itself, not as being able to constitute the world as it chooses.

Althusser's 'anti-humanism' had its roots in the philosophy which he developed to replace, or overcome, that of Sartre. The dominant theme in Sartre's existentialist philosophy, for example, had been that human consciousness was free to choose. By this Sartre meant that human beings were free in the sense that nothing, such as unconscious desires or economic modes of production, could be held to fully determine human choices. Althusser, in contrast to Sartre, insisted upon the constituted nature of subjectivity and of human consciousness.[1] If human subjectivity is constituted, not constitutive, then it follows that it is the processes involved in the constitution of subjectivity by external structures such as language, political institutions and economic forces, which have to be understood in the social science of Marxism. This structuralist view was to replace the existentialist position that consciousness was to be seen as a free entity able to choose how to see and constitute the world for itself, unaffected by external or internal forces.

The critique of the Althusserian problematic has turned on the degree to which it is possible to invest Marxist 'scientists' with privileged access to knowledge based upon 'science' as distinct from everyone else's 'ideology'. Such a view as that held by Althusser appeared to many to be over-dogmatic, difficult to state in a coherent form, and potentially totalitarian.

Only those who understood Marxism as a science could analyse modern capitalism and decide, presumably, what it was possible for a political party to do in given circumstances.

Althusser's position also rested upon what has been termed a 'statist' conception of power. Such a viewpoint holds that power is located in the state and its various components, from the armed forces and the police to schools and churches — called by Althusser the 'repressive state apparatuses' and 'ideological state apparatuses' respectively. This viewpoint was criticized, implicitly at least, in the work of Michel Foucault. Foucault conceptualized power as diffused throughout society, not only in the state and its various apparatuses. For Foucault, wherever there was a 'discourse' in place there power was to be seen being exercised. If Althusser over-estimated the role of the state, especially in the conceptualization of 'ideological state apparatuses' which, to say the least, did not make it easy to see how any forms of dissent could ever develop, Foucault might be said to have under-estimated the state in an over-diffuse conception of power.

Both of these positions failed to conceptualize the role of human agents in the processes of change. Althusser and his critics, such as Foucault, emphasized one side only of the continuum of constituted–constitutive subjectivity. In these theories subjects were seen as constituted by processes which they could not control. However this is not the position Marx held, at least as far as Gramsci was concerned. Gramsci had emphasized both the constituted and the constitutive aspects of human agencies of change in Marx's work. The dismissal by Althusser of the theory and philosophy of the early Marx for being too humanistic, preoccupied with Hegelian categories such as consciousness, dialectics, and alienation, has had serious consequences for reading the later Marx of *Das Kapital*, and the middle Marx of the *Grundrisse*, as will be discussed later.[2] Gramscian Marxism contains both the notion that classes are constituted by the dominant mode of production and that groups other than classes may become potential agents of change, that is, able to aim at constituting their economic and political world. National-popular movements were a specific example Gramsci gave of such non-class-based agents of historical and political change.

Nevertheless there can be no question of simply returning to Marx, Lenin or even Gramsci. For in spite of the continuing presence of world capitalism, the situations in which Marx, Lenin and Gramsci each worked differ from that prevailing in the world in the period since nineteen-fifty. Features such as the affluence of many people in Western capitalist societies, the existence of nuclear weapons, the disappearance of the European empires, the continuing capacity of capitalism so far to avoid major collapse as a world economic system, the negative aspects of actually existing socialist societies, such as the lack of freedom to create in the arts, to travel, to discuss and form social movements, plus the knowledge about the Gulag, all these features have altered millions of people's understanding of the world since Gramsci's lifetime. It has become plausible to think that no longer do the words 'socialism', let alone 'communism', suggest something worth striving for to many young people in the Western world, but rather something which is not much fun and is to be avoided. It is sometimes claimed by right-wing politicians that it is the Western, and more specifically the American, way of life which many people, especially young people in Western and Eastern Europe, Australia, New Zealand, and in some parts of Latin America, Asia and Africa, wish to emulate. The American way of life appears to offer the promise of more excitement together with possibilities for personal and social change and development. It appeals to many people as the more desirable system when compared with Soviet or Chinese socialism. This whole train of argument suggests that the Western way of life has achieved hegemony, in the sense of active consent, among significant groups of people throughout the world — including many living under actually existing socialism.

However, there is something mistaken in this kind of usage of the term 'hegemony'. It is odd to say that a partial outlook upon the world such as that of liberal, individualistic hedonism can be 'hegemonic'. The concept of hegemony is not a value-neutral term within a positivistic social science. Rather in Gramsci's work, the concept of hegemony is linked with a complex set of claims about what could be a coherent viewpoint on the world. In this perspective only a coherent world-view, a well-rounded philosophy and related morality, could be hegemonic. This does not mean that there is one universally valid position, valid that is for all times and places, but that at any given stage of historical development a particular philosophical world-view may provide the major way of grasping what is going on in the world and of living creatively in it. In earlier periods, for example, Catholicism and Protestantism could be said to have been 'hegemonic' in particular societies in the sense that they were important world-viewpoints, philosophically and morally well developed as outlooks on all spheres of social action, including the political, military, familial, aesthetic, and economic, which were widely accepted by the population in countries influenced by one or other of these viewpoints.

Liberalism could be said to have been hegemonic in the past too, especially in the English-speaking world. It generated a world-view, a theory of political economy, which was philosophically and epistemologically grounded, together with ethics and political values, and became popularized among millions of people. As was mentioned earlier it has had something of a revival in the United States, Britain, West Germany and

France in the early nineteen-eighties under the label of the 'New Right'. This economic form of liberalism has tried to remove the state from the operation of economic markets — in investment, production, consumption, employment and currency movements for instance — but has not been able to sustain complete non-interventionism by the modern state and central banks. Nor has this form of non-interventionist liberalism been able to sustain hegemonic leadership in Britain for it has not been able to attain the position of being taken for granted as 'the obvious way to run things' even within the Conservative Party.

In its political form, however, liberalism still exercises a strong attraction among many people in the West. This aspect of liberalism stresses: the freedom from unnecessary state interference in the lives of ordinary citizens; freedom of expression in speech, in broadcasting, in the arts and in publications; freedom to organize in social movements and to dissent openly from the government. Some people living under actually existing socialism, deprived of the liberal freedoms of expression, are attracted to political liberalism. Even in Western capitalist countries, including Britain, these liberal political freedoms still have to be fought and struggled for if they are to be maintained; they are not attained once and for all. In many of the countries under world capitalism's influence, such as South Africa, the Philippines under Marcos, and Argentina under the colonels, these liberal freedoms have never existed for most of the population. The population of Hong Kong cannot decide on their own government under the British administration, yet this colony is held up by some of the New Right as an example of the virtues of free market capitalism, unfettered by high government taxation and state interference. There can be no plausible claim, therefore, that free market capitalism guarantees wider cultural and political liberties, as Hayek and others, such as Milton Friedman, have argued, if one looks at these examples.[3] On the other hand there has been no example, up to the present time, of a fully socialist economy which is seen as clearly providing and guaranteeing these cultural and political freedoms to all citizens.

The approach which will be taken here to the wider problematic in which the concept of hegemony is located leads to an examination of the relations between philosophy and social theory in Chapter 3. The view that these two disciplines are logically and inextricably involved with one another, and that this affects the analysis of hegemony, will be explored in that chapter. I will argue that philosophy is concerned both with epistemological issues and with examining the claim that political and ethical values can be discussed rationally.[4] Any social theory has to make some set of epistemological assumptions and has to take some view about how political and ethical values are to be formed. This is as true of positivistic social theory, especially as this is to be found in much sociology, as it is of those social theories, such as critical theory and phenomenological approaches, which are more prepared to see their relationship with philosophy as a close one. I shall argue that in the discussion of hegemony, especially in the work of Gramsci, the relationship between philosophy and social theory is of central importance.[5] This is partly because the concept belongs to a philosophy/social theory — Gramscian Marxism — and partly because the concept refers to philosophies, or world-views, as being hegemonic or not and this involves discussion about what is to count as philosphy. Such a discussion is itself philosophical — part of a necessary conceptual analysis of the meaning of the term 'philosophy'. Gramsci's social theory of hegemony involves philosophical assumptions about epistemology, and about political and ethical values, which have to be addressed.[6]

I shall begin, however, by outlining the concept of hegemony as this can be found within Gramsci's work. The early traces of the concept in the work of Marx and Lenin will be discussed. There are problems with reaching a view about exactly what Gramsci's position was on hegemony. This issue is addressed in chapter 1. In Chapter 2 the basic problematic which underlies the concept of hegemony in Gramsci is discussed. This involves, it will be argued, both a social theoretical aspect and a moral/political philosophical component. The issues raised by this problematic, of which the concept of hegemony forms the central focus, concern the relationship between moral/ political philosophy, social theory, and the social sciences. These issues are discussed in Chapter 3. The work of Max Weber, which I argue has some similarities to the Gramscian enterprise, despite their political differences, is discussed in Chapter 4. More recent discussions about hegemony, its role in social theory and as a guide to political action in contemporary Western Europe, are analysed in Chapter 5. In the Conclusion some of the more contemporary political implications of the analysis of the concept of hegemony given in the book will be discussed.

REFERENCES

[1] See T. Benton, 'The Contradictions of Althusser', in *Ideas from France. The Legacy of French Theory*, edited by L. Appignanesi, London, ICA, 1985, p. 35.

[2] See D. McLellan, *Marx's Grundrisse*, London, Macmillan, 1971.

[3] See, for example, F. Hayek, *The Road to Serfdom*, London, Routledge & Kegan Paul, 1944; and F. Hayek, *The Constitution of Liberty*, Chicago, 1960.

[4] See the interview with J. Habermas, 'A Philosophico-Political Profile', in *New Left Review*, No. 151, 1985, pp. 75–105.

[5] See also C. Buci-Glucksmann, *Gramsci and the State*, translated by D. Fernbach, London, Lawrence & Wishart, 1980.

[6] On the philosophy/social theory relation see A. Giddens 'Reason without Revolution?' Habermas's 'Theorie Des Kommunikativen Handelns', in *Praxis International*, **2**, No. 3, 1982, pp. 318–338.

1

The concept of hegemony

The work of Antonio Gramsci, the Italian Marxist, has been important in the social theory developed by some recent Marxists and by those calling themselves 'post-Marxists'. The concept of hegemony was the central, most original, idea in Gramsci's social theory and philosophy. It is helpful and important, therefore, to trace the idea of hegemony as it developed within Gramsci's work and to locate it within Marxism, both before and after Gramsci. This will involve an understanding of the kind of problems the concept was used to handle by Lenin and Gramsci, and in more recent contributions such as that made by the 'post-Marxists' E. Laclau and C. Mouffe.

The recent recovery of the concept of hegemony within Marxism/post-Marxism is important also in assessing the criticisms which some sociologists have made of Marxism — criticisms such as that Marxists artificially isolate the economic base from culture and politics; that they make this 'economic base' a determining factor of what goes on in political and other social institutions in a way which fails to give sufficient autonomy to the political and cultural spheres.[1] Many contemporary Marxists, however, influenced by the Gramscian concept of hegemony, do not now maintain an economic determinist position. It is no longer possible, therefore, to counterpose sociology and Marxism as differing over economic determinism.

Gramsci's work has been central in the emergence of a new form of Marxist theory, especially in Italy, since the end of the Second World War. Gramsci had worked as a journalist from 1916; in 1921 he had become a member of the central committee of the newly formed Italian Communist Party and was elected its leader in 1924 on his return from a visit he had made to Moscow. Gramsci was imprisoned soon afterwards in 1926 by Mussolini, who had seized power in Italy in 1922. Gramsci remained in prison for the rest of his life, being allowed out from prison to die in hospital. His prison writings, published in English as *Selections from the*

Prison Notebooks (1971), were written under the difficult conditions of prison censorship.[2] Before his imprisonment he had been a participant in the workers' occupation of the Turin factories in late 1920. His writings of this period, mainly of a journalistic variety, are of some help in trying to work out the effects of the prison censor on Gramsci's prison writings.

The experience with the worker's councils in Turin helped to shape Gramsci's later views about party leadership and its relationship to the masses, views which differed greatly from those who stressed party discipline and centralism. Gramsci was concerned with people giving their full understanding and consent to the policies which political leaders aimed to carry out. This was in sharp contrast to those who were concerned primarily that members obeyed directives and orders from a central committee. He argued that it was important to establish this mutually reciprocal relationship between leaders and the masses before a revolution, for otherwise, after any revolution, the relation between government and people would become dictatorial. The concept of hegemony which Gramsci developed meant, in part, that people of all non-exploiting classes should give their consent to the philosophy of praxis, as Gramsci called Marxism, as a result of education and understanding, not through processes of manipulation and imposition by a party elite.

Before Gramsci, the concept of hegemony had not been a central one in Marxist social theory. It was never an explicit concept in Marx. The conceptualization of the state in Marx's work which is relevant to the notion of hegemony, and the state/civil society distinction, will be discussed, however, in the next section of this chapter.

THE LATENT NOTION OF HEGEMONY IN MARX

Marx had experienced the repressive impact of Prussian state censorship during his early work as a journalist on, and editor of, the German magazine *Rheinische Zeitung*; the Prussian censor's ban on the magazine eventually caused him to move to Paris in 1843. The theme of alienation, which Marx considered in the *Economic and Philosophic Manuscripts of 1844*, included the idea that the state could be seen as a form of alienation, a component of man's self-estrangement, along with religion, labour, money and property. Marx had written:

> The positive abolition of private property as the appropriation of human life, is thus the positive abolition of all alienation, and thus the return of man from religion, the family, the State, etc., to his human, i.e. social, life.[3]

These manuscripts were almost certainly unknown to Gramsci, being published in Russian in 1927, and other languages in 1932, whilst Gramsci was imprisoned.[4] Gramsci's problematic of hegemony was seen therefore as being untainted with these early, humanistic, Hegelian-influenced, non-scientific papers produced by the young Marx, in the eyes of Althusserian Marxists. This has helped the assimilation of Gramscian Marxism among some structuralists and post-structuralists anxious to eschew the humanism of the early Marx.

Marx's ideas on the state were never fully developed — he had planned a volume of *Capital* on the state but never wrote it — and this left what was to prove to be a serious lacuna in Marxism.[5] It has also to be remembered that neither the working classes nor women voted in elections, nor could these major groups participate in trade union and political activities, in the early part of the nineteenth century when Marx began writing. The state, in the countries of Western Europe during Marx's lifetime, was not the modern state of the early twentieth century which Gramsci knew. Furthermore the development of Welfare States in Western Europe, the establishment of new state governmental systems in Italy, West Germany, and France at the end of the Second World War, and the end of colonialism, all these events have made significant differences to the state known not only by Marx, and Lenin, but also by Gramsci.

The remarks which Marx had made about the state were understood by most later Marxists in an instrumentalist way, based upon a mechanistic and economistic distinction between the economic base and the ideological superstructure. The state was seen as only an arm of class rule, not as an autonomous, or relatively autonomous, sphere. As the French writer, C. Buci-Glucksmann, has argued:

> As against all reductionist conceptions of the state (the state as a neutral repressive instrument in the hands of a class-subject who wields it), Gramsci conceives the role and presence of the state in the relations of production of civil society . . . .[6]

The way in which Marx is understood to have seen the state and its role in a capitalist society depends upon the theoretical and philosophical position of the reader. This truism is important in grasping the shifting understandings of Marx both within European Marxism and in mainstream Western sociology during the twentieth century, particularly since the nineteen-thirties. During periods when a form of positivism has been a dominant philosophical tendency Marx has been read as a scientist who developed theoretical laws from which empirical predictions about capitalist crises and revolution could be deduced. When existentialism was predominant in post-war Europe, then the more 'humanistic' Marx was emphasized — the Marx of alienation, praxis, and 'revolution' seen as the return of man's essence to himself.[7] Under the impact of critical theory the idea of Marxism as a critique of bourgeois consciousness, as a dialectical philosophy emphasizing the need for activity and thought which was a negation of the present situation, was emphasized. The role of Reason in historical development became important for critical theorists, as in the work of Herbert Marcuse for example.[8]

Althusser's reading of Marx, which was developed in the nineteen-sixties and -seventies, criticized the existentialist and critical theoretical interpretations of Marx as being Hegelian and, therefore, pre-scientific versions of Marxism. Althusser emphasized the scientific aspect of Marx's work, eschewing all concern with concepts such as those of alienation, dialectics, reason and history, as all being Hegelian and therefore 'pre-Marxist'.[9] The science which Marx founded had developed only after he had made an epistemological break with Hegelian philosophy and with the political economy of Adam Smith and other economists. The form of social theory which is the central concern here, namely that centred around the idea of hegemony, is not as concerned to be 'scientific' as Althusser was in his heyday. Rather the new form of Marxism is preoccupied with political issues in Western Europe particularly. It is concerned with developing a social theory for the analysis and understanding of contemporary forms of modern capitalism in which the criteria of judgement are less those of the pure 'scientificity' of conceptual developments than philosophical, moral leadership and political relevance.

If any specific writings of Marx have been significant in the development of the centrality of hegemony in Gramscian Marxism then it has been *The Eighteenth Brumaire of Louis Bonaparte* (1852, second edition 1869) and *The Class Struggles in France 1848–1850* which would seem to have had a central part to play. One British writer, Stuart Hall, has argued:

> It is above all [in these two texts] that the concepts begin to emerge which enable us to grasp the sources and the mechanisms of the 'relative autonomy' of the political level of the class struggle from the economic.[10]

For Marx, in these texts on France, the figure of Napoleon came to represent not the interests of the bourgeoisie in any direct sense but those of the large number of conservative peasants. Napolean had claimed to be above class interests and to represent the interests of the 'nation'.[11] However, the state bureaucracy which Napolean set up, on the basis of the taxation of the small-holding peasants, came to serve the interests of the maturing capitalist relations in France. It helped provide the surplus population with jobs, to develop coercive repression of sections of the population, and to form the executive power of the state without interference from the parliament.[12] The political sphere thus can be seen as relatively autonomous, but nevertheless as linked in with the economic interests of the capitalists, even if this was indirect in form, in this analysis provided by Marx.

The concept of 'civil society' as a distinct site of social relations and actions was lost in the work of Althusser and his followers. The concept was not one, however, which had been rejected by Marx for being over-Hegelian, even though a concept of civil society did exist in Hegel. Rather Marx had transformed the concept as found in Hegel to use it for his own purposes, as in *The Eighteenth Brumaire*. For example Marx distinguished the notions of state and civil society in that text:

> The State enmeshes, controls, regulates, supervises and regi-ments civil society from the most all-embracing expressions of its life down to its most insignificant motions, from its most general modes of existence down to the private life of individuals.[13]

In this proposition the state acts in what might be termed a totalitarian way upon civil society. Conceptually, however, the two are separated before the state comes to dominate. The loss of the concept of civil society in Althusser has been a problem for without it there is no way of maintaining a non-statist approach to hegemony. Without the notion of civil society as separate from the state the concept of hegemony can come to seem totalitarian in its effects — which is something it was not in Gramsci.

Before discussing these matters further it is necessary to look briefly at the work of Lenin on hegemony, for this influenced Gramsci's work particularly as a means of clarifying his own distinctive ideas.

LENIN

The notion of hegemony was first produced in the eighteen-eighties by the Russian Marxists, especially by Plekhanov in 1883–84. It had been developed as part of the strategy for overthrowing Tsarism. The term referred to the hegemonic leadership the proletariat, and its political representatives, should give in an alliance of other groups, including some bourgeois critics, peasants and intellectuals who were seeking an end to the Tsarist police state.[14] It was in this context that Lenin formulated the ideas which appeared in *What is to be Done?* in 1902. In this text Lenin discussed the problems of the political education of the workers. He wrote, for example:

> however much we may try to 'lend the economic struggle itself a

political character' we shall never be able to develop the political consciousness of workers . . . by keeping within the framework of the economic struggle, for that framework is too narrow.[15]

To bring political knowledge to the workers the Social-Democrats must go among all classes of the population . . . .[16] [And this must be as] theoreticians, as propagandists, as agitators and as organisers.[17]

The advance which Lenin made over previous discussions of the idea of hegemony, as can be seen from these remarks, was to stress the role of theoretical leadership. He argued also that: '. . . the role of vanguard fighter can be fulfilled only by a party that is guided by the most advanced theory'.[18]

Theory is essential, in Lenin's view, if trade union consciousness is to move beyond being enslaved by bourgeois ideology.[19] Lenin quotes Engels, from a piece Engels had written in 1874, to the effect that the German workers were the most theoretically minded in Europe:

Without German philosophy which preceded it, particularly that of Hegel, German scientific socialism . . . would never have come into being. Without a sense of theory among the workers, this scientific socialism would never have entered their flesh and blood as much as is the case. What an immeasurable advantage this is may be seen, on the one hand, from the indifference to all theory, which is one of the main reasons why the English working-class movement crawls along so slowly in spite of the splendid organisa-tion of the individual unions; on the other hand, from the mischief wrought by Proudhonism, in its original form, among the French and Belgians . . . .[20]

Lenin saw the state as an instrument of class rule. He wrote after the 1917 Revolution as follows:

The state is the product and the manifestation of the irreconcilabi-lity of class antagonisms. The state arises when, where and to the extent that class antagonisms objectively cannot be reconciled.[21]

Lenin expected that the state would eventually wither away, but not that this would occur immediately after the Russian Revolution. He hoped that revolutions would break out in Germany and elsewhere in Europe after the First World War ended. The failure of the German revolution to emerge, the rise of Nazism, the second 'great Patriotic War', followed by the Cold War, all these events have served to maintain a strong state presence in the Soviet Union since the time of Lenin and Gramsci.

The analysis Gramsci had given of the Russian Revolution in 1917 involved seeing it as a 'war of manoeuvre', that is a 'war of movement', in a society which had a low level of development of the institutions and organizations of the type found in the 'civil society' of Western European countries, especially in Britain and France. The Russian state had been capturable by a sustained attack upon it in the capital, Saint Petersburg, in a way that was not possible in Western Europe, Gramsci argued. Civil society was almost non-existent in Russia, especially in the period of the First World War. Once state power was taken by the Bolsheviks, they could try to maintain their position by using the state's coercive forces against those aristocratic and bourgeois elements seeking to overthrow the revolution, both within Russia and outside it, and by effecting changes in education, in places of work and in the press. This second process was an attempt to build up the hegemony of the proletariat within the new system.

Gramsci's advance over Lenin was to develop a strategy for use within Western European societies, based on the distinction he made between a 'war of movement', which had been possible in Russia in 1917 and which had been based upon a direct assault on the state, and a 'war of position' which was applicable in Western Europe. In a war of position the aim would be to try to achieve hegemony for the proletariat in civil society before the capture of state power by the Communist Party. This distinction between a war of manoeuvre and a war of position has to be understood in the light of Gramsci's wider theoretical concepts as will be discussed below. It must be remembered that Gramsci developed the strategy of a war of position both before and during the fascist period in Italian political history, otherwise his ideas can be misinterpreted if they are removed from this context.

Gramsci used the concept of hegemony to describe and analyse how modern capitalist societies were organized, or aimed to be organized, in the past and present. The bourgeoisie had exercised hegemonic leadership relatively successfully in Britain, in civil society, in the state and in the economy. In France after the Revolution of 1789, Gramsci argued, the bourgeoisie had ruled hegemonically too. By contrast, the northern Italian bourgeoisie, based in Piedmont, had failed to exercise hegemony in Italy and consequently the Italian state remained vulnerable to the fascists because it was not based upon the hegemonic leadership by the bourgeoisie in either civil society or in the state.

There has been confusion here about the concepts involved, for Gramsci seems to have first distinguished the state from civil society, the state being defined as the source of coercive power in a society and civil society as the site of hegemonic leadership. However, he went on to link these two concepts together to define what he termed 'the integral state' as the combination of hegemony armoured with coercive power. The integral state is 'political society plus civil society, in other words, hegemony protected by the armour of coercion'.[22] The integral state, as Gramsci conceptualized it, had two aspects: the means of coercion (police force and army); and the means of establishing hegemonic leadership in civil society (education, publishing, broadcasting and cinema). R. Simon has pointed out that Gramsci was trying to show that 'the social relationships of civil society are relations of power just as much (though in a different way) as are the coercive relations of the state'.[23]

The concept of the 'integral state' can be distinguished from that of totalitarianism. There is no element of voluntary agreement in totalitarianism as there is in an integral state, where agreement about basic goals is based upon a common set of ideas and values, a common philosophy shared by most people on the basis of active, freely-given consent. Consent is not manipulated nor produced by fear of coercive force, nor does the state fuse with the institutions of civil society, in an integral state as in totalitarianism. An integral state would not imprison opponents who argued against it as the fascist regime imprisoned Gramsci. In order to unravel the notions of an 'integral state' and civil society, it is useful at this point to examine the important work of Perry Anderson on Gramsci's *Prison Notebooks*.

THREE MODELS IN GRAMSCI

In a seminal article, published in 1977, Perry Anderson argued that there were three distinct models in Gramsci's *Prison Notebooks*. He argued that none of the models was entirely satisfactory from either an analytical or political point of view.[24] In Gramsci's first model hegemony, in the sense of cultural and moral leadership, was seen as being exercised in civil society; the state was the site of coercive power in the form of the police and the armed forces; and the economy the site of work disciplines, the cash nexus and monetary controls. The problem with this model, Anderson argued, was that hegemony was very much exercised in the state in Western bourgeois democracies in the form of parliamentary democracy. Most members of the working class believed that they did exercise a choice about their rulers by voting in elections. This consent is of a qualitatively new type from that given in previous societies. Although Gramsci saw 'consent' as crucial, paradoxically he 'never produced any comprehensive account of the history or structure of bourgeois democracy in his *Prison Notebooks*'.[25]

In the second model, hegemony was seen as being exercised in the state as well as in civil society. Gramsci came to see the crucial importance of educational and legal institutions in the exercise of hegemony. Schooling and policing were crucial activities in the building of hegemony in Western Europe during the early part of the twentieth century; they were increasingly activities of the state, however, not of civil society. The notion of the moral and ethical leadership of the state, which the Italian philosopher Croce developed, influenced Gramsci's thinking here. Gramsci wrote for instance that:

> Every State is ethical in so far as one of its most important functions is to elevate the great mass of the population to a given cultural and moral level, a level or standard which corresponds to the needs of development of the forces of production and hence to the interests of the dominant classes. The school as a positive educational function and the courts as a negative and repressive educational function are the most important such activities of the State: but in reality a multiplicity of other so-called private initiatives and activities tend towards the same end, which constitute the apparatus of political and cultural hegemony of the ruling class.[26]

This aspect of the second model Gramsci developed was reasonable, in Anderson's view at least. But it was linked with a confusing addition, namely that hegemony also included physical coercion in the form of the activities of the police and prisons, with the introduction of the law into the model. Anderson argued that this model entailed that hegemony was not seen as being limited to moral and philosophical leadership alone but involved a coercive element. This was, however, a confusion of precisely the distinction between hegemony and coercion so central to the whole Gramscian enterprise as I will present it in the next chapter.[27]

The third model lost the distinction between the state and civil society altogether, for Gramsci sometimes defined the state as 'political society' plus 'civil society' as in the following quotation for example:

> by the 'state' should be understood not only the apparatus of government, but also the 'private' apparatus of 'hegemony' or civil society.

> hegemony . . . belongs to private forces, to civil society — which is 'State' too, indeed is the State itself.[28]

Anderson concluded that 'the distinction between State and civil society is cancelled'.[29] This has had grave consequences in the way Gramsci has been used by Althusser, who rejected the notion of 'civil society' in his work. Althusser subsumed too much under the two aspects of the state, the 'repressive state apparatuses', which did derive from and link with Gramsci's notion of coercion in the state, and the concept of 'ideological state apparatuses' which lost the autonomy the notion of civil society originally had in Gramsci.

Perry Anderson also argued that the *Prison Notebooks* were difficult to read for two reasons. The first reason was that Gramsci had to think his ideas within concepts provided by past thinkers, just as Marx had had to do. In Marx's case the major thinkers whose ideas he used and criticized had been Hegel, Ricardo, Adam Smith, and Proudhon. In Gramsci's case they were Machiavelli and Croce. One might add Lenin too, for his thought had a strong influence on Gramsci. Nevertheless Gramsci moved beyond Lenin both theoretically and politically in his conception of a 'war of position'. Not only is Gramsci's writing, like that of most original thinkers, based upon other writers' conceptualizations in the first instance, but his *Prison Notebooks* have a second and more unique feature which makes them more difficult to interpret accurately than other texts, namely that they were written so that could pass through the prison censorship. This means that the text of the *Prison Notebooks* is full of ellipses, disorders, allusions, repetitions, spaces and contradictions, or so Anderson claims.[30]

These points are important to bear in mind in reading Gramsci's *Prison Notebooks* but it is not easy, even if it is possible, ever to reconstruct the original intentions of any writer. A text is made useful by later generations because people bring their own conceptions, hopes, needs, values and political purposes to bear on it. The meaning of the text is constructed but not merely read off as part of an objective exercise of reading a text. However, the meanings which can be read in a text are neither infinite in number nor arbitrary in character. Reading is not an exact science, but it is not as arbitrary as deciphering the meaning said to be found in the stars' positions, or in tea-leaves in a cup, for example. Reading Gramsci's *Prison Notebooks* is certainly especially difficult because of the presence of the prison censor, but Gramsci had written other pieces before being imprisoned and the sense of the prison writings can be related to those produced outside of prison. This is something which has been done by Christine Buci-Glucksmann (1980) for instance, since the article produced by Perry Anderson in the mid-nineteen-seventies, which was restricted to an analysis of the *Prison Notebooks*. [31]

In the light of later Gramsci scholarship it is clear that some major assertions which Anderson made need correction. Anderson wrote:

the characteristic medium in which Gramsci presented his ideas was that of a protocol of general axioms of political sociology, with 'floating' referents — sometimes allusively specified by class or regime or epoch, but equally often ambiguously evocative of several possible exemplars. This procedure, foreign to any other Marxist, was of course dictated by the need to lull the vigilance of the censor . . . The mask of generalization into which Gramsci was thus frequently driven had serious consequences for his thought: for it induced the unexamined premise that the structural positions of the bourgeoisie and the proletariat, in their respective revolutions and their successive states, were historically equivalent.[32]

There is, however, no necessary connection between writing in prison conditions, trying to dodge the censor, being unable to obtain certain Marxist books, and a 'fault' in a basic conceptual issue of the kind which Anderson argues Gramsci made. Anderson held that Gramsci mistakenly assumed that the proletarian revolution would be structurally similar to the bourgeois one. Gramsci's work, written both before he was imprisoned and during his imprisonment, points to exactly the opposite conclusion. Gramsci is precisely concerned with the differences between the way the bourgeoisie came to power in France and Italy on the one hand, and with the differences between a successful bourgeois revolution, such as the French or the British ones, and on the other hand a revolution based on the proletariat in alliance with other groups.

In later exegesis of Gramsci's work, both the *Prison Notebooks* and his earlier political writings, which was made by Anne Showstack Sassoon, there is a consistent case put forward that Gramsci was concerned with the difference between various bourgeois revolutions in history (especially the Italian one, which was not successful hegemonically and led to the possibility of fascism taking over the state) and a revolution in Western Europe led by the proletariat.[33] She argued that for Gramsci:

The proletariat cannot found a state on the same basis as the bourgeoisie . . . First of all, the proletariat is founding a state to do away with all exploitation in the Marxist sense, whereas the bourgeoisie were replacing one form of exploitation with another. From his earliest work, Gramsci argues that the working class has as its historical project the creation of a new type of state, in which the very concept of politics is transformed as the masses intervene and control politics and economics . . . Furthermore, Gramsci argues throughout his work that an integral state can only be founded if a class enjoys hegemony before it achieves state power . . . All this implies widespread popular consent.[34]

How could Anderson produce such a different reading? It is because his notion of a proletarian revolution is different from that of Gramsci or certainly different from that of many Gramscian Marxists in Western Europe in the nineteen-eighties. Anderson argued:

The logic of Marxist theory indicates that it is in the nature of the bourgeois State that, in any final contest, the armed apparatus of repression inexorably displaces the ideological apparatuses of parliamentary representation, to re-occupy the dominant position in the structure of capitalist power. This coercive State machine is the ultimate barrier to a worker's revolution, and can only be broken by pre-emptive counter-coercion.[35]

Later on Anderson argued:

It is probably the case that the majority of the exploited popula-tion in every major capitalist social formation today remains subject in one way or another to reformist or capitalist ideology.[36]

It is here that Gramsci's problematic of the United Front is very relevant today in North America, Japan and Western Europe. The masses in these societies 'have yet to be won over to revolutionary socialism in their plurality'.[37] This struggle to win the convictions of the working class must be achieved before there can be any talk of winning state power in its coercive sense, Anderson argued.

Capitalists must sleep easier after reading this for the convictions of the working class are not seen as being much of a problem to the bourgeoisie, both because the size of the classic nineteenth and early twentieth centuries industrial proletariat is shrinking in modern capitalism in the United States and Western Europe and because the convictions of people are in any case not something manipulated by capitalists, or put into the minds of the masses by them, but rather they flow from the exigencies of everyday life under capitalism. The workers, and others, hold the values and political ideas that they do as a consequence of both trying to survive, and of attempting to enjoy themselves, within capitalism. These activities require money; the cash nexus remains, therefore, a major means of social, economic and political control. The control exerted by the cash nexus is mediated by ideological means, for people have to come to desire the goods offered for sale. Such desires are not natural nor inborn, and they are not taken for granted by modern capitalism. The desires to consume various products have to be constructed by ideological apparatuses, especially in the mass media — not only by explicit advertisements but more especially through the portrayal of life-styles in stories, films, articles, photographs and television images. No revolution led by the proletariat of the Western capitalist societies is in sight on this view, as long as their desires to consume goods and services are being formed in these ways. In order to consume it is necessary to earn money or to obtain cash from the state. These exigencies produce conformity among most citizens in the modern states of capitalism.

In addition peace, and the avoidance of nuclear war, have become prime objectives in the eyes of most people in the West. A violent revolution to institute socialism/communism in place of Western capitalism has come to appear undesirable and even unthinkable in these societies.

HEGEMONY IN GRAMSCI

Three major terms identify discrete, albeit interconnected, areas in a social formation which form the baseline for the conceptualization of hegemony. These three terms, which have been mentioned above, are: the economic, the state, and civil society. It is the emphasis which Gramsci gave to the state, or the political, and to civil society, which distinguishes his work from that of other major Marxist writers. This emphasis did not exclude the economic but has served to help Marxism to move away from being a form of economism — that is the view that the economic base determines the ideological superstructures of religion, politics, the arts, law or education. Briefly the three major terms can be defined as follows.

The 'economic' is the term used to connote the dominant mode of production in a territory at a particular moment in time. This consists of the technical means of production and the social relations of production which are built upon the differential ways classes are related to the ownership of the means of production, as either substantial owners, or as non-owners who are employed in organizations concerned with production.

The 'state' consists of the means of violence (the police and armed forces) in a given territory, together with state-funded bureaucracies (the civil service, legal, welfare and educational institutions).

The term 'civil society' connotes the other organizations in a social formation which are neither part of the processes of material production in the economy, nor part of state-funded organizations, but which are relatively long-lasting institutions supported and run by people outside of the other two major spheres. A major component of civil society so defined would be religious institutions and organizations, apart from entirely state-funded and state-controlled religious organizations.[38] The major means of communication which are not under state censorship, or political control, might also be seen as part of civil society, although their status can be ambiguous in that newspapers may be owned by capitalists, and some broadcasting systems may be dependent upon state funding, either directly or indirectly, as in the case of the British Broadcasting Corporation. Many other organizations are formed outside of state bureaucracies and are funded by voluntary contributions, especially in the English-speaking world and in Scandinavia. These include: women's organizations from Women's Institutes to the more recent Women's Movement; youth groups; sports clubs; groups concerned with the natural environment; and many arts and entertainment organizations which are not state-funded nor directly controlled by the state politically. The borderline between state and civil society is a constantly shifting one and one which has to be negotiated, maintained and continually re-adjusted over time. Nevertheless, this does not affect the importance of the analytical distinction between the two sites of action.

As always with any such classification as the one just outlined, it must be remembered that the categories are analytical and that, therefore, empirically any particular organization may change its location over time, or belong to two, or all three, of the analytically distinguished sectors. There can be legitimate debate about where to place any specific organization. These analytical distinctions are important ones to make, however, in social theory. They might also make a claim to being an exhaustive set in that they can include all major forms of social action — politics, legal activities, economic action, education, cultural activities generally, religion, the family, gender and sexuality, and the mass media.[39]

It is not only the distinctions between the three analytical elements which matter in social theory but also the specification of their interrelationships. There has been great difficulty in finding any satisfactory way of expressing the relationship between these three elements, the debates having moved from rigid economic determinism at one end of the continuum of possibilities, in which the economic base is seen as determining the ideological superstructure defined as consisting of the state and civil society, to the conception of the three elements being independently variable, or completely autonomous of one another, at the other end of the continuum.[40] The attempt to develop an intermediate position, of the type which specifies that the economic is determining 'in the last instance', but that otherwise there is a considerable degree of relative autonomy of the state and civil society from the economic, has not been easy to sustain because such a position tends to gravitate to one pole of the continuum or the other. Either the economic element does operate in some determining and specifiable way to affect the activities of the state and the organizations of civil society, or the state, and/or the components of civil society, can produce changes in the economic area.

These issues have been raised before. Max Weber, the German sociologist, raised similar but not identical issues about economistic Marxism to those of Gramsci. The similarities and differences between Gramsci and Weber will be discussed in more detail in Chapter 4. Here it is important just to note the existence of these different positions. The claim will be developed later that they are dissolved by the problematic of hegemony.

The originality of the Gramscian concept of hegemony stems, in large part, from the break it produced away from dogmatic Marxism's approach, an approach which saw Marxism as being only a theory about economically determined classes and their actions. In Gramsci's view the dogmatists' attempt to turn Marxism into a mechanistic, deterministic and positivistic scientific schema, led to an over-emphasis upon the economic sphere and the class analysis derived from that in terms of 'relationship to the means of production'. This form of Marxism assumes that once a change in the ownership of the main economic means of production, distribution and exchange has been accomplished there will be no major obstacles to a truly democratic, and free, society. In Gramsci's view this was mistaken, for it neglected the other major areas of society, namely the state and the institutions of civil society.

By opposing economism, Gramsci sought to emphasize the political. This was not to the exclusion of the economic area, nor of economic classes, but to include the state and civil society as areas in which power was exercised and hegemony established.

A central concept in this zone of struggle for hegemony was that of the nation — hegemony means leadership of the people of all classes in a given nation-state. This can never be achieved by narrow economic–corporate actions by those in power in the state system on Gramsci's view. The 'people' must be addressed — 'hailed' as Althusser put it — in order to emphasize the creative, constitutive aspect of addressing the 'people'. Such an emphasis should not be allowed to obscure the processes whereby 'a people' can come to constitute themselves, however, apart from being addressed by those from outside it as members of the same 'people'.

Ethnic identity is in part constituted by religious leaders, who themselves may emerge from the group in question, and who help to create specific ethnic–religious groups which may think and feel themselves to be separate from others in the same state territory, as with the Mormons, the Ras Tafarians and the Jews, for example.[41] There is also a secular element in such identity construction, often expressed and created in folk customs, dance, song, literature, both written and oral, and in games and sports. The boundaries of these ethnic groupings may or may not coincide with the boundaries of a modern state.

The notion of the 'nation state' suffers from being both a conflation of two distinct concepts and from leading to an under-emphasis upon the problems of matching the boundaries of self-constituted ethnic groups with those of a state territory. 'State' and 'nation' are two analytically distinct concepts which are often distinct empirical entities too within world politics. In Gramsci's terminology it could be said that the 'nation', and other ethnic identities, are constituted in 'civil society'; the 'people' are constituted in part in the educational system, as in the teaching of the specific language, literature, geography and history of 'our' country or of 'our' people. The state, as a coercive apparatus, controls the laws and the administration of 'justice' in a given territory; such a body of law helps to constitute 'a people' who are subject to it.

These two components — state and national, ethnic group — may conflict, as they have often done in the past and continue to do in the later part of the twentieth century, as in Spain, France, Britain, Ireland and in divided Germany. The educational system of the state may try to impose a collective sense of being members of a 'people' which is in contradiction with the notions about national identity children have picked up in the culture of their ethnic group in 'civil society'.

In the construction of national identities by states, and of ethnic identities among 'peoples', intellectuals defined in a broad sense so as to include doctors, teachers, priests, judges, lawyers, writers, politicians, artists, philosophers, journalists and broadcasters, can play a crucial role. Technicians, managers, and civil servants, who were included also in the category of 'intellectuals' by Gramsci, typically play a less crucial role in these matters concerned with the construction and maintenance of national and ethnic identities.[42] Gramsci thought that many Marxist intellectuals, however, had become cut off from popular national sentiments. He was anxious to emphasize the need for such intellectuals to experience the feelings of the people, and not remain abstract pedants:

> The popular element 'feels' but does not always know or under-stand; the intellectual element 'knows' but does not always understand and in particular does not always feel . . . The intellectual's error consists in believing that one can know without understanding and even more without feeling and being impassioned (not only for knowledge in itself but also for the object of knowledge): in other words that the intellectual can be

an intellectual (and not a pure pedant) if distinct and separate from the people-nation, that is without feeling the elementary passions of the people, understanding them and therefore explaining and justifying them in the particular historical situation and connecting them dialectically to the laws of history and to a superior conception of the world, scientifically and coherently elaborated i.e. knowledge. One cannot make politics–history without this passion, without this sentimental connection between intellectuals and people–nation. In the absence of such a nexus the relations between the intellectual and the people–nation are, or are reduced to, relationships of a purely bureaucratic and formal order; the intellectuals become a caste, or a priesthood . . . .[43]

Only if this relationship between intellectual leaders and the people–nation, between rulers and ruled, is one of 'organic cohesion in which feeling–passion becomes understanding and thence knowledge (not mechanically but in a way that is alive), then and only then is the relationship one of representation'.[44]

Hegemonic leadership involves developing intellectual, moral and philosophical consent from all major groups in a nation. It involves an emotional dimension too, in that those political leaders who seek hegemonic leadership must address the sentiments of the nation–people and must not appear as strange or alien beings who are cut off from the masses. The implications of this kind of conception of hegemony for more theoretical issues, especially the relationship between philosophy and social theory, will be explored further in Chapters 2 and 3.

REFERENCES

[1] P. Worsley has written:
It is my contention that the model of base and superstructure which most Marxists, including Marx, took as the key image through which to express the essence of their theoretical system, is in fact quite incompatible with the idea of a dialectical science of society, since it implies not only conceptually isolating the economy in an unacceptable way, but also assumes that the latter somehow is necessarily more decisive than anything else.
P. Worsley, *Marx and Marxism*, Chichester and London, Ellis Horwood and Tavistock Publications Limited, 1982, p. 113.
[2] A. Gramsci, *Quaderni del Carcere* (1929–1935), six volumes, edited by V. Gerratana, Einaudi, Turin, 1948–51.

The quotations in this book are from A. Gramsci, *Selections from the Prison Notebooks*, edited and translated by Q. Hoare & G. Nowell Smith, London, Lawrence & Wishart, 1971 (=SPN).

[3] K. Marx, *Economic and Philosophic Manuscripts* (1844); from T. Bottomore & M. Rubel, *Karl Marx. Selected Writings in Sociology and Social Philosophy,* Harmondsworth, Penguin, 1971, p. 250.

[4] I. Meszaros, *Marx's Theory of Alienation,* London, Merlin Press, 1970, p. 11.

[5] See D. McLellan, *The Thought of Karl Marx*, London, Macmillan, 1971, Part Two, chapter 6.

[6] C. Buci-Glucksmann, *Gramsci and the State*, translated by D. Fernbach, London, Lawrence & Wishart, 1980, Preface to the English-language edition, p.x.

[7] For example, J.-P. Sartre, *Critique of Dialectical Reason,* Translated by A. Sheridan-Smith, London, New Left Books, 1976.

[8] H. Marcuse, *Reason and Revolution*, Oxford, Oxford University Press, 1941.
H. Marcuse, *One Dimensional Man*, London, Routledge & Kegan Paul, 1964.
H. Marcuse, *Counter-Revolution and Revolt*, London, Allen Lane, The Penguin Press, 1968.

[9] L. Althusser, *For Marx*, London, Allen Lane, 1969. L. Althusser, *Lenin and Philosophy and Other Essays*, London, Verso Press, 1977.

[10] See S. Hall, 'The "Political" and the "Economic" in Marx's Theory of Classes' in *Class and Class Structure*, edited by A. Hunt, London, Lawrence & Wishart, 1978, pp. 19–54. Reprinted in R. Bocock *et al., An Introduction to Sociology*, London, Fontana, 1980, pp. 197–237. Quotation from p. 219 of the Fontana paperback edition.

[11] See S. Hall, op. cit. in ref. [10] above, pp. 225–227.

[12] Ibid., p. 227.

[13] K. Marx, *The Eighteenth Brumaire of Louis Bonaparte* (2nd edition, 1869), reprinted in K. Marx, *Surveys from Exile*, London, Harmondsworth, Penguin, p. 186.

[14] See P. Anderson, 'The Antinomies of Antonio Gramsci', in *New Left Review*, No. 100, 1976–77, p. 15.

[15] V. I. Lenin, *What is to be Done?* (1902), Moscow, Foreign Languages Publishing House, p. 132.

[16] Ibid., p. 133.

[17] Ibid., p. 138.

[18] Ibid., p. 41.

[19] See ibid., p. 67.

[20] F. Engels quoted by Lenin, ibid., p. 42–43.

[21] V. I. Lenin, *The State and Revolution*, 2nd edition, Moscow, Foreign Languages Publishing House, 1918, p. 12.

[22] A. Gramsci, SPN, p. 263.

[23] R. Simon, *Gramsci's Political Thought. An Introduction,* London, Lawrence & Wishart, 1982, p. 72.

[24] P. Anderson (1976–77), op. cit. in ref. [14] above.

[25] Ibid., p. 31.

[26] A. Gramsci, SPN, p. 258.

[27] P. Anderson, op. cit. in ref. [14], pp. 32–33.

[28] A. Gramsci, SPN, p. 261.

[29] P. Anderson, op. cit. in ref. [14].

[30] P. Anderson, ibid., p. 6.

[31] C. Buci-Glucksmann, op. cit. in ref. [6] above.

[32] P. Anderson, op. cit. in ref. [14], p. 20.

[33] A. Showstack Sassoon (ed.), 'Passive Revolution and the Politics of Reform', in *Approaches to Gramsci*, London, Writers and Readers, 1982, p. 141.

[34] Ibid., p. 141.

[35] P. Anderson, op. cit. in ref. [14].

[36] Ibid., p. 78.

[37] Ibid., p. 78.

[38] A. Gramsci, SPN, p. 245, on Church/State/civil society.

[39] See P. Anderson, op. cit. in ref. [14] above, on the problems of distinguishing civil society and the political in Gramsci. Also A. Showstack Sassoon's reply in the book edited by her *Approaches to Gramsci*, 1982, London, Writers and Readers, 'Hegemony, War of Position and Political Intervention', p. 105.

[40] See, for example, L. Althusser, *For Marx*, London, Allen Lane, 1969; and M. Weber, *The Protestant Ethic and the Spirit of Capitalism*, translated by T. Parsons, London, Unwin University Books, 1971, p. 26 of the Introduction.

[41] See M. Yinger, *The Scientific Study of Religion*, New York, Macmillan, 1970, Chapters 12, 14 and 15.

[42] See R. Simon, *Gramsci's Political Thought. An Introduction,* London, Lawrence & Wishart, 1982, Chapter 12, 'The Intellectuals'.

[43] SPN p. 418.

[44] SPN p. 418.

2

Gramsci's problematic

Gramsci's work on hegemony was never systematically outlined in the *Prison Notebooks*. As was discussed in the first chapter, this has meant that the issue of where hegemony is exercised on Gramsci's view, whether in civil society, the economy, the state, or in some combination of these, is a matter of debate and interpretation. For such an interpretation to be adequately based it is important to try to reach an appreciation of the wider theoretical framework, or problematic, Gramsci developed in order to place the concept of hegemony within it. The term 'problematic' is used here to mean a social theoretical position which is linked, either explicitly or implicitly, to a broadly based philosophical viewpoint. By placing the concept of hegemony in this wider context, it becomes easier to see what Gramsci hoped to achieve with it.

In this chapter two major aspects of Gramsci's overall position are discussed, namely his critique of economism on the one hand, and his relationship to the philosophy of Croce, the Italian philosopher, on the other. This discussion, in turn, prepares the ground for a wider and more detailed exploration of the relations between philosophy and social theory, in the light of the concept of hegemony, in Chapter 3.

ECONOMISM

The major theoretical position within Marxism which Gramsci sought to correct was that of economism. In part Gramsci was following in the footsteps of Lenin in so doing. Lenin, as was discussed in the last chapter, had criticized economism and trade union consciousness in the first two or three years of the twentieth century. He had been particularly concerned with the practical effects of economism on the development of the struggle to overthrow Tsarism in Russia. Lenin had portrayed the limitations of trade union consciousness alone. In *What is to be Done?* (1902) Lenin wrote:

The history of all countries shows that the working class, exclusively by its own effort, is able to develop only trade union consciousness, i.e. the conviction that it is necessary to combine in unions, fight the employers and strive to compel the government to pass necessary legislation etc. The theory of Socialism, however, grew out of the philosophic, historical and economic theories that were elaborated by the educated representatives of the propertied classes, the intellectuals.[1]

Lenin also had attacked 'economism' for belittling the importance of the ideological struggle for the minds of workers, and allowing them to fall under the influence of bourgeois ideology.[2] Such criticisms had been made by Marx and Engels, so that a plausible case can be made that Lenin's stress upon the need for theory did have some claim to be a consistent development of Marx's thought.[3]

Marx too had criticized trade unions at the end of the eighteen-seventies. Writing, for example, in *Wages, Price and Profit* Marx had said:

Trades Unions work well as centres of resistance against the encroachments of capital. They fail partially from an injudicious use of their power. They fail generally from limiting themselves to a guerilla war against the effects of the existing system, instead of simultaneously trying to change it, instead of using their organized forces as a lever for the final emancipation of the working class, that is to say, the ultimate abolition of the wages system.[4]

There is here an assumption that trades unions have a potential for achieving change, if only they would act in ways which would change the wages system, that is abolish the system of extracting surplus value from labour. Marx did not develop his political thinking on how this was to be done in any great detail. If trades unions operated as they did because of the constraints of the situation in which they found themselves, as Marx suggested, then it is not clear how this could be altered from within trade unionism. Some new influence would be required from elsewhere if change in trades unions' consciousness was to occur. Hence Lenin's development of the practical political idea that a group should seek to educate trade unionists out of their limited consciousness seems to be an inevitable development of the analysis Marx began.

Gramsci drew upon Lenin but he extended his arguments into a wholly new perspective, a new social theory and political practice, a new problematic. He developed the critique of economism begun by Marx and Lenin as he interpreted their work and sought to adapt this critique to the conditions prevailing in Western Europe during the nineteen-twenties and -thirties.

What is the position which is termed 'economism', and which Gramsci aimed to correct? Economism maintains that there is a contradiction within capitalism over the material, economic, interests of the proletariat and those of the capitalist class, or class fractions, which will lead eventually to the total breakdown of the capitalist economic system, which is based upon profit and the extraction of surplus value from the industrial working class. This breakdown will occur independently of the intentions of either of the two major classes involved. In one, early, version of economism, the assumption was that the proletariat would become more and more impoverished, and revolt against their miserable situation. Marx and Engels's proposition in the *Communist Manifesto* (1848) about the increasing misery of the proletariat under capitalism, which would lead that class to turn to revolution, was understood as a simple statement about the increasing economic poverty of the working classes by those holding an economistic viewpoint. This economistic interpreation was linked with a mechanistic, and deterministic, approach to political and historical change. The revolution, to be made by the proletariat, was seen as inevitable; a necessary outcome of capitalism's crises. Comrades had to await the revolutionary situation, and be ready to act when it arrived. There was little they could do until the time of revolution. One major consequence of this analysis was what Gramsci termed a 'fatalist' approach in both political and industrial trade union affairs; the major stance was one of waiting for the revolution to happen.

Economistic interpretations of Marx, furthermore, have underestimated the more philosophical aspects of his work. Gramsci's term for Marxism, namely the philosophy of praxis, does serve to make clear that it is philosophy which is of paramount concern. Furthermore, for Gramsci, unlike Althusser, the philosophy in Marx is a form of humanism. On Gramsci's view Marx had held that people were impoverished as human beings under capitalism. They were restricted in their development, partly as a consequence of the rigid division of labour, and partly as a result of a lack of full relationships with other people under conditions of long hours of work in exploitative situations. The increasing misery and impoverishment of the proletariat has a different meaning on this interpretation from that of material poverty. The 'increasing misery of the proletariat' does include material poverty, but it also means the impoverishment of a human being's capacities for development and creativity, something which may occur even in relatively affluent material conditions.

In what the French Marxist philosopher Louis Althusser regarded as a pre-scientific text, *The Holy Family* (1845), Marx had written:

> If socialist writers attribute this world historical role (of making the revolution, RJB) to the proletariat this is not at all, as the 'Critical School' tends to believe, because they regard the proletarians as gods. On the contrary, in the fully developed proletariat, everything human is taken away, even the appearance of humanity. Man has lost himself, but he has not only acquired, at the same time, a theoretical consciousness of his loss, he has been forced . . . by practical necessity — to revolt against this inhumanity.[5]

This same theme persists into, for example, *Capital*, Volume 3, (written 1867 onwards; first published 1893–94) where Marx writes of establishing in modern industry:

> such conditions as are proper and worthy for human beings. Nevertheless, this always remains a realm of necessity. Beyond it begins that development of human potentiality for its own sake, the true realm of freedom, which however can only flourish upon that realm of necessity as its basis. The shortening of the working day is its fundamental prerequisite.[6]

The conceptions of human potentiality and its converse, human impoverishment, remained in Marx's work from the early to the late writings. Remove the humanism in Marx's works, as Althusser proposed and insisted upon doing, and the major motivation lying behind Marx's analysis of capitalism is lost.

Both Gramsci and Lenin were still old-fashioned enough to think that Marxism was a philosophy as well as a social theory within political economy — 'old-fashioned' because it is often assumed in the modern era that philosophy is finished as an independent basis of knowledge and theory, and as a foundation for political economy. This is a mistaken view, as I hope to show in the next chapter. For the moment, the point to note is that economistic interpretations of Marxism are a major object of criticism for both Lenin and Gramsci. The need to emphasize Lenin in this context is because the Stalinists in the Soviet Union claimed to be Leninists, indeed to be the guardians of his mind and thought as well as of his mortal remains, yet lost his emphasis upon the need to win the struggle for people's hearts and minds. The assumption seemed to be that this was no longer necessary in the Soviet Union after the revolution, and that Lenin's position in *What is to be Done?* applied only before a revolution. Even so, in the West, the need to struggle philosophically remained for Gramsci. The non-economistic, non-deterministic, and philosophical aspects of Lenin have been lost in the communist world as a consequence of Stalinism. The work of Gramsci has enabled some to see a different side to Lenin, a 'Gramscian' aspect to him.

This stress upon continuities between Lenin and Gramsci has had political importance for those writing for the French Communist Party, particularly, in order to legitimate Gramsci as a key guide and thinker, in the post-Althusserian phase. Althusser has provided a non-historicist, non-Hegelian, version of Marxism, and he had used a modified version of the concept of hegemony.[7] In the Italian Communist Party there has been less of a problem in moving away from Stalinism because Gramsci was that party's founding father. In other Western European communist parties, in Spain for example, Gramsci has had an easier entry than in France. The British Communist Party has become more and more 'Gramscian', less and less Stalinist, during the late nineteen-seventies and early nineteen-eighties, although economistic positions still persist in the British Communist Party and elsewhere on the Left in Britain.

There has been a lack of understanding of the proper relationship between philosophy and social theory, both in political economy and sociology, within economistic circles on the European left and in some academic works. For example, the editors of *Karl Marx. Selected Writings on Sociology and Social Philosophy*, T. Bottomore and M. Rubel, in spite of the title of their book, wrote in their Introduction:

> Modern sociology is not the sociology of Marx, any more than it is the sociology of Durkheim, or Weber, or Hobhouse. It is a science which has advanced some way towards freeing itself from the various philosophical systems in which it originated, and with which its founders were still embroiled.[8]

This notion that it is an improvement for modern sociology to be non-philosophical is, I believe, not only potentially disastrous for sociology and philosophy but is logically unviable. It is potentially disastrous because it leads to a situation in which disputes in sociology, such as those between phenomenological sociologists and positivists, or Weberians and Marxists, are conducted too often as disputes within sociology, whereas they are based upon differences in philosophy and epistemology. The result of the failure to locate differences in epistemology and ethics between sociologists within philosophical discourse has been, all too often, intellectual muddle.

It is in any case logically unviable to try to maintain a rigid separation between sociology and social theory on the one hand, and philosophy on the other, because the basic concepts used in social theory need to be derived from philosophical positions, not only in epistemology, although this is of crucial importance, but also with regard to concepts such as those of human action, choice, moral values, language and meaning. Because the relationship between philosophy and sociology/social theory is so funda-mental, it is mistaken to treat their separation as an advance. It is a positivist error to try to maintain a rigorous separation between these disciplines. These points will be further developed in the next chapter.

Gramsci had argued that Marxism, 'the philosophy of praxis', cannot be divided into

> two parts: a 'sociology' and a systematic philosophy. Separated from the theory of history and politics philosophy cannot be other than metaphysics, whereas the great conquest in the history of modern thought, represented by the philosophy of praxis, is precisely the concrete historicisation of philosophy and its identi-fication with history.[9]

To return to the issues raised by Gramsci's critique of economism. It is not only the working class which can fail to escape an economic-corporate position, that is one in which its own fairly immediate economic interests form the basis of its outlook, its political and economic actions. Any class, or alliance of classes and class fractions, may do this. The northern Italian bourgeoisie had acted entirely as an economic-corporate interest group and thereby failed to establish hegemonic leadership in the state or civil society of Italy, on Gramsci's analysis. The French and British bourgeoisies did establish a more successful hegemonic leadership role after their revolu-tions against the landed aristrocracies of their respective societies. The North American bourgeoisie had not had a well-established aristocracy to overcome, once the British were successfully opposed as the imperial power in 1776. The north-eastern industrial bourgeoisie finally achieved dominance in the state and economy after the American Civil War in the early eighteen-sixties.

Hegemonic leadership may entail that policies have to be pursued at times which are in the interests of the whole people, the nation, and not in the narrow interests of the bourgeoisie, or some dominant fraction of it. It was just this that the northern Italian bourgeoisie had failed to do. Gramsci emphasized this point in order to combat the narrow perspective of economism as a theoretical position. However, this did not mean that he lost sight of the economic interests of the dominant group in a state. He wrote for instance:

> Undoubtedly the fact of hegemony presupposes . . . that the

leading group should make sacrifices of an economic-corporate kind. But there is also no doubt that such sacrifices and such a compromise cannot touch the essential: for though hegemony is ethical-political, it must also be economic, must necessarily be based on the decisive function exercised by the leading group in the decisive nucleus of economic activity.[10]

Nevertheless, I think that for Gramsci hegemonic leadership fundamentally involved producing a world-view, a philosophy and moral outlook, which other subordinate and allied classes, and groups, in a society accepted. Gramsci searched North American literature, for instance, for signs that the bourgeoisie of the United States had been able to move beyond their economic-corporate stage and act as world leaders in the area of philosophy. He concluded in the *Prison Notebooks* that the dominant class in the United States . . .

> had no real superstructure, no cultural self-consciousness, no self-criticism. [America] had not yet created a conception of the world and a group of intellectuals leading the people in a framework of civil society . . . .[11]

One major reason for this failure of the Americans to lead hegemonically, which some people think still continues in the nineteen-eighties, is that the United states has not produced a world-view, a philosophy, which has moved beyond positivism and empiricism. Even American pragmatism, which Gramsci admired, had failed to break through the anti-intellectual, positivistic, and at the same time, at a more popular level, naively religious, culture of the United States. Philosophy, in the Gramscian sense of a coherent world-view and morality, is not thought to be a viable intellectual activity in the United States, therefore it cannot produce such a philosophy and lead the western world 'hegemonically'. To many Western Europeans, and to many educated people in other parts of the world too, American philosophy is virtually non-existent. In spite of some valuable contributions to linguistic philosophy made by American philosophers, its overall culture appears to many European intellectuals to be vulgar and philistine. This may appeal to uneducated groups in the world, but a country cannot be hegemonic if it fails to lead the educated, cultured groups too. Without hegemonic consent and leadership, a country such as the United States in the post-World War Two situation can only use coercive military force, or economic power, to impose its will, or to try to manipulate situations for its own narrow economistic purposes. This only serves to further weaken its stading among those educated groups it needs to lead morally, philosophically and culturally if it is ever to achieve full hegemony in world capitalism.

Before considering the issues concerning philosophy and social theory in a more general way, it is important to examine the critique Gramsci gave of the philosophy of Croce. This is necessary because some dogmatic Marxists, for example, have held that Gramsci remained trapped in the philosophical idealism he had learned from Croce and that consequently he cannot be counted as a 'Marxist' in their view.[12] To assess this kind of claim, some discussion of Croce is required.

CROCE AND IDEALISM

The Italian philosopher Benedetto Croce (1866–1952) dominated the intellectual life of his country during the early part of the twentieth century. Croce had been a Marxist for a few years between 1895 and 1900, whilst influenced by the Marxist philosopher Antonio Labriola (1843–1904), before becoming a more Hegelian philosopher of history. Labriola had used the phrase 'philosophy of praxis' to describe Marxism, a term which Gramsci later resurrected. Gramsci paid Labriola's student, Croce, more detailed attention, however, seeing him as the twentieth-century equivalent of Hegel, given the influence Croce came to exert over Italian thought in the early nineteen-twenties. Croce had been extremely critical of positivism and scientism, especially for the anti-ethical influence he claimed this type of outlook produced.

Croce not only wrote philosophy, he was politically active too. He had become the Italian Minister of education in the Giolitti government of 1920. Croce was at first sympathetic to the Mussolini regime, which came to power in 1922, even though he was not a fascist. He had hoped to moderate the influence of the fascists and to insert an ethical dimension into Italian politics. As a well-known figure in Italy and abroad, the fascist government were not able to attack him too openly, nor to imprison him.

For Gramsci, the similarity between Croce and Hegel consisted not just, or even primarily, in the fact that Croce was Hegelian, but in the intellectual influence and significance of their respective philosophies. Croce was the dominant philosopher of his time, at least in Italy, and as such Gramsci argued that he had to be addressed critically, just as Marx had developed a critique of the dominant philosopher of his period, Hegel. Croce has been seen as an 'idealist' philosopher, a view Gramsci might have shared but only after careful consideration of his work. However, Croce's philosophy cannot be grasped adequately as being a simple form of idealism. To see why this is so, it is necessary to discuss and define the term 'idealism' first, and after this has been done the nature of Croce's philosophical position may be compared with other forms of idealism.

The term 'idealism' is used in this context to mean a position which emphasizes the role of ideas and moral values in the understanding and explanation of major historical changes. Moral values and ideas are held to be the most important factor in motivating people to act historically in order to try to achieve a better world. This view can be contrasted with 'materialism' which holds that actions which lead to major changes in history are produced by the material, economic interests of classes. Idealists have been criticized by materialist Marxists as being too unrealistic in their estimation of what it is really possible to achieve in a given situation. In the view of materialist Marxists, such as the Russian philosopher Plekhanov (1857–1918), for example, idealism underestimated the importance of material, economic, determinations which operate in all historical situations. It is the material interests of classes which cause historical changes.

The positions both of idealism and of materialism were rejected by Gramsci and, he argued, by Marx. The position which Marx developed was one of 'dialectical materialism', which tried to preserve the 'active side' of idealism, that is the role which human consciousness plays in conceiving of ways of transforming nature and society and which tried to avoid the purely passive role attributed to the mind in non-dialectical forms of materialism. Marx had argued in the *Theses on Feuerbach*, a text to which Gramsci referred, that:

> The chief defect of all previous materialism . . . is that things, reality, the sensible world, are conceived only in the form of objects of observation, but not as human sense activity, not as practical activity, not subjectively. Hence, in opposition to materialism, the active side was developed abstractly by idealism, which of course does not know real sense activity as such.[13]

Marx and Gramsci both aimed to emphasize the material, practical side of human projects, unlike idealist philosophers, such as Hegel and later Hegelians, who remained at a very abstract level of philosophizing, and did not try to achieve their ideals, their projects, their moral values, in real historical circumstances.

Marx had continued in the *Theses on Feuerbach* as follows:

> The question whether human thinking can pretend to objective truth is not a theoretical but a practical question. Man must prove the truth, i.e. the reality and power, the 'this-sidedness' of his thinking in practice. The dispute over the reality or non-reality of

thinking that is isolated from practice is a purely scholastic question.[14]

For Marx, therefore, practical activity was the only way of knowing truth, especially in the area of history-making, or politics.

Returning to Croce, it is important to point out here that he held an epistemological position which posited that human beings cannot know that there is an external world behind our perceptions of it; we can only know the contents of our minds, of our consciousness. In Croce's view it is not logically legitimate to posit the existence of a Kantian 'noumenon' behind the 'phenomenon' that we do experience. Nor can we know that there is another world, a metaphysical one in which a God exists. Both this metaphysical view, and the claim that Kantian noumena exist, are claims to know 'transcendental' objects which cannot be known. All that can be known has to come through action in history, where 'history' is understood as a widely defined term to mean the changing world of both nature and society. Croce's political activity was, therefore, an essential part of his philosophy — for only in this way could theories be tested, or verified. In this way his philosophy cannot be called simply 'idealist' without some qualification. Croce emphasized that historical changes came about as a result of human action and will, of political action, and not as the by-product of some inevitable processes akin to those which produced change in the natural world.

Croce came quite close to pragmatism in his solution to the problem of knowledge. Technology, including the initial form of testing in the laboratory, was seen as the site for testing and generating knowledge in the natural sciences. Similarly in the areas of history and politics, it was actions which changed historical circumstances which provided the test of knowledge in the social sciences. Croce developed the idea that philosophies too are tested in history, that a philosophy which enabled a person or group to attain changes in historical, political, circumstnces was *ipso facto* a good, or adequate, philosophy. Pragmatism holds that if predicted changes result in the world as a result of applying a particular theoretical schema to a phenomenon, via technology or political actions, then that theoretical schema may be accepted as true. Croce seemed to hold a similar, if not identical, view to this.

The problem with pragmatism as a satisfactory epistemological position, however, is that some theories 'work' in the required sense, that is they produce results, or their predictions come true, but they seem to be highly implausible in other respects. They may be, for instance, internally incoherent, or they may clash with other well-founded and coherent views about the world. This is the case with witchcraft, for example, which may yield more accurate predictions and results than would be expected by chance, but its own accounts of how and why it works remain implausible on other grounds. The idea that there are forces of good and evil in the universe, which can be manipulated by witchcraft to produce a desired result, does not fit with our other rationally founded views about the world and the universe as a system. This later view has no place for such additional forces of a magical type, manipulable by some human beings through spells, potions or talismans.

Some criterion of rationality, such as that of the internal consistency of a theory, seems to be required, either in addition to pragmatic criteria, or instead of them. Gramsci's stress upon the intellectual coherence of a world-view can be seen as a recognition that pragmatism, of the Crocean variety, was not in itself enough in judging philosophies. Success in gaining political power, for instance, could not be used as an adequate way of choosing between different political philosophies. The criterion of the degree of rational coherence of a philosophy was used in judging world-views by Gramsci, together with a judgment about the moral goals and the means used to attain them in a given political philosophy. Fascism in Italy could be criticized from Gramsci's position but Croce was unable to do this. Croce had been at first a supporter of this form of political philosophy. This was a perfectly consistent position for Croce to hold if the sole criterion of judging a political philosophy was that it could attain office and so be able to effect changes through action.

Croce held that philosophy was concerned with human consciousness because it was consciousness which constituted the world. The natural and social–historical worlds did not simply impinge on human consciousness, as in empiricism, but they had to be actively grasped. Croce held that there were two major types of activity of concern to philosophy which enabled humans to grasp the world:

first, intellectual activity, which has two forms:
(a) intuition — concerned with the concept of beauty; studied by aesthetics;
(b) abstraction — concerned with the concept of truth; studied in what Croce called logic.
second, practical activity, which also has two forms:
(c) economic activity — involving the concept of utility; studied by economics.
(d) ethical activity — involving the concept of goodness; studied by the discipline of ethics.[15]

Philosophy could work out its truth only in historical judgements in Croce's view. History is bound up with life, with action, with practicalities, and it is in relationship with these that knowledge can be tested. Croce wrote:

> In point of fact all concrete knowledge whatever is on a par with historical judgement, bound to life, that is to action, of which it marks a pause or an anticipation having for its function to break down . . . any obstacles barring a clear view of the situation from which it must specifically and with determination emerge.[16]

Gramsci took seriously Croce's emphasis upon the constituting role of human consciousness. This does not imply that there is complete freedom to perceive the world independently of pre-given categories, or that the external world can be constructed in any way an individual or group chooses. The relationship with history, with the material world, prohibits this totally idealist interpretation in both Croce and Gramsci. It does imply that people collectively can form projects for change and act to try to achieve them — either in technology or in political activities. The given historical situation, with its specific technological, economic, and political circumstances operates to limit what can be done. Some projects for change remain, therefore, utopian, unrealistic, while others do express real possibilities for change. A social theory is needed to help in the assessment of actions which seek to change political, historical, or cultural circumstances. Social theory, on Gramsci's view, can guide groups in assessing which actions may succeed, and which may fail, in bringing about the objectives which a group has in particular countries and in specific circumstances.

In the end Gramsci came to view Croce as a 'speculative' philosopher whose claims to link philosophy and history were never put into concrete form.[17] They remained abstract and not linked up with any concrete and effective political programmes for change. Croce's political activities failed to achieve major changes of the kind his philosophy required — changes in morality, away from the use of physical violence and force by political movements or by the state, towards an 'ethical state', that is a state which educated its citizens into a moral system which eschewed the use of violence. Fascism proved to be too strongly committed to the use of force and physical coercion for Croce to be able to influence it in a moral direction, towards building an 'ethical state'.

Gramsci came to think that only a strong political party, the Communist Party, based upon the industrial working class, intellectuals, artists and peasants, could provide the required resistance to fascism. Gramsci concluded that philosophy and morality had to become collective property; the individual philosopher, such as Croce, was ineffective in twentieth-century conditions. The 'Modern Prince' has to be a party, not an individual, in modern conditions.

In the early work of Gramsci there had been a strong moral element which he had derived in part from Croce. Human beings were seen as capable of making their own history; neither God, nor the Absolute of Hegel, nor objective historical laws, govern history — man makes his own history, and could potentially govern the process. This involved Gramsci in critiques of both religious views of history, especially that of Roman Catholicism, and those of positivism in its various guises. One of the guises positivism had taken, Social Darwinism, saw history as a process involving wars, conflicts between species, and by extension and false extrapolations, of one nation, or 'race', against another nation or race. Positivism also appeared in Marxism itself, as in the works of Plekhanov and Bukharin, where iron laws of historical development were posited which would lead inevitably to the downfall of capitalism and the arrival of socialism. Gramsci opposed such views, as will be discussed later, and in their place asserted that people could and should take control of history by political actions which would realize a new kind of hegemonic civilization, based upon a philosophical world-view — the philosophy of praxis — with a new economic and political order in line with the philosophy.

Such a position is not best described as being 'idealist', for Gramsci held that concrete political actions were necessary to try to achieve the changes thought possible and necessary for men and women to develop their creativity. This contrasts with Croce's position which did not advance to an adequate political position, even though as was seen above, Croce held that philosophy can only be tested in history. Gramsci also argued that it was necessary to know the economic, political and military situation in any given society before embarking upon fruitless adventures, in which the workers' movement could be broken, workers and their leaders shot or imprisoned, and the cause of socialism put back for many years.[18] For this task a social theory was essential, to serve the philosophical goals held by a political movement aiming at change and trying to establish a new hegemonic world-view.

The originality and strength of Gramsci is that he held that some ethical element was needed in Marxism, and that some vision had to be put forward of a possible set of changes to be attained through concrete political actions. The content of a political programme would vary depending upon the place and time of the group seeking changes in accordance with the most advanced philosophical view possible — derived from the philosophy of praxis. As one recent writer, J. Femia, has written:

If, as Gramsci believed, socialism was not inscribed in the logic of history, then it must be based on an ideal goal, on a vision of what 'ought-to-be'. The open and indefinite perspective of the 'ought-to-be' replaces the closed chain of determinism. As long as the relationship between man and reality is not a passive, scientific one, the dimension of the 'ought-to-be' is intrinsic to politics.[19]

Gramsci did not deviate from this view that Marxism was a doctrine 'more concerned with the full development of all human faculties than with economic contradictions'.[20] For Gramsci, Marxism was not only a tool of analysis, or a guide to political action, it was also a whole new philosophy, a new conception of the world. This being so, 'neither political economy nor sociology could provide an adequate theoretical basis'.[21] Marxism was a new moral philosophy for Gramsci, and this ethical dimension was in part produced by his critical study of Croce. Unlike Croce, Gramsci saw the need for collective political organization if a new moral philosophy was to become hegemonic.

Philosophy, therefore, becomes an indispensable term at this point if we are to grasp the full meaning of the social theoretical concept of hegemony, for it involves the central idea of moral and philosophical leadership in a society. In Chapter 3, therefore, the relations between philosophy and social theory will be discussed in detail.

REFERENCES

[1] V. I. Lenin, *What is to be Done?* (1902), Moscow, Foreign Languages Publishing House, p. 50–51.

[2] See ibid., pp. 63–68.

[3] See C. Buci-Glucksmann, *Gramsci and the State*, London, Lawrence & Wishart, 1980.

[4] K. Marx, *Wages, Price and Profit*, First published 1898, Moscow, Foreign Languages Publishing House, p.94–95.

[5] K. Marx, *The Holy Family,* First published in 1845, London, Lawrence and Wishart. See quotation in T. Bottomore & M. Rubel, *Karl Marx on Sociology and Social Philosophy,* Harmondsworth, Penguin, 1971, p. 237.

[6] K. Marx, *Capital,* volume 3. First published by F. Engfels, 1893–4, London, Lawrence and Wishart. See quotation in T. Bottomore & M. Rubel, op. cit. in ref. [5], p. 260.

[7] See C. Buci-Glucksmann, op. cit. in ref. [3] above, p. 72.

[8] T. Bottomore & M. Rubel, op. cit. in ref. [5], p. 63.

[9] A. Gramsci, *Selections from the Prison Notebooks,* edited and translated by Q. Hoare & G. Nowell Smith, London, Lawrence & Wishart, 1971, p. 436.

[10] Ibid., p. 161.

[11] A. Gramsci, Notebook 5, p. 105. Quoted in C. Buci-Glucksmann, op. cit. in ref. [3] above, p. 319.

[12] See J. Femia, *Gramsci's Political Thought. Hegemony, Consciousness and Revolutionary Process,* Oxford, Clarendon Press, 1981, p. 62.

[13] K. Marx, *Theses on Feuerbach*, the first thesis. The Theses can be found in T. Bottomore & M. Rubel, op. cit. in ref. [5] above, pp. 82–84.

[14] Ibid., p. 82 (Second of the 'Theses on Feuerbach').

[15] See M. White, *The Age of Analysis*, Mentor, New York, 1955, p. 46.

[16] B. Croce, *History as the Story of Liberty*, London, Allen & Unwin, 1941 p. 33–34; first published in Italian as *La Storia come Pensiero e come Azione*, 1938.

[17] See J. Femia, op. cit. in ref [12] above, p. 97.

[18] Ibid., chapter 3, pp. 87 & 121, for a discussion of Gramsci on Rosa Luxemburg.

[19] J. Femia, op. cit. in ref. 12 above, pp. 121–122.

[20] Ibid., p. 122.

[21] Ibid., p. 122.

3

A new problematic

The new problematic centring upon the concept of hegemony raises two fundamental questions: first, how should we conceive of the relationship between philosophy and the social sciences in general; second, how should we conceive of the relationship between moral/political philosophy and sociology in particular? These questions will be explored in this chapter. After an examination of some of the general issues involved has been made in the first section, more specific reference will be made to Marx and later Marxism in the second and third sections in examining the second question.

PHILOSOPHY AND SOCIOLOGY

The starting assumption which I shall make here for the purposes of the discussion about the relationship between philosophy and the social sciences is as follows: in the past a useful, working relationship between philosophy and the social sciences has been arrested by the various forms of positivism which have been developed in both subject areas. The social sciences, especially in the English-speaking world, have been defined as positivistic sciences by many of their practitioners, that is as being discourses in which value judgements are eschewed, and in which theoretical propositions are regarded as empirically verifiable or falsifiable. Given such a self-definition it is difficult, if not impossible, for social scientists to grant much significance to philosophical discourse, which is seen as being characterized by propositions which are not empirically testable and are therefore devoid of interest or meaning. Philosophy has frequently been seen by social scientists as being concerned with value judgements and, therefore, as being outside the concerns of the value-neutral social sciences.

This picture of philosophy, however, does not accurately depict much of the philosophy which has been produced by English philosophers since the mid-twentieth century. This type of philosophy has sought to avoid making

value judgements too, just like social scientists. Rather linguistic philosophers have been concerned to analyse the concepts of moral discourse,
often to make the important point that moral judgements are logically
possible, as against the earlier logical positivistic view of the Vienna Circle
that value statements are, strictly speaking, meaningless. Later linguistic
philosophers have avoided making detailed value judgements themselves,
however, with some notable exceptions as in the work of Rawls.[1] The
major task has been seen as one involving the analysis of fundamental
moral concepts such as 'goodness', 'duty', 'justice', 'rights', 'liberty', and
'ought' for instance, and examining how they function in ordinary language. But this kind of discussion may leave unexamined, and uncriticized,
value judgements which are contained in ordinary language at any given
point in time.

The work of Rawls has marked a break with this kind of approach. He
has not only sought to analyse concepts but has also aimed to establish what
a theory of justice ought to contain. To aid him in this task he used the
Kantian concept of autonomy arguing that:

> Moral philosophy becomes the study of the conception and
> outcome of a suitably defined rational decision . . . Kant held, I
> believe, that a person is acting autonomously when the principles
> of his action are chosen by him as the most adequate possible
> expression of his nature as a free and equal rational being. The
> principles he acts upon are not adopted because of his social
> position or natural endowments, or in view of the particular kind
> of society in which he lives or the specific things that he happens to
> want. To act on such principles is to act heteronomously.[2]

Rawls developed his theory of justice in purely philosophical terms, i.e.
on the assumption of rational autonomy. Given this way of defining his task
Rawls made no use of sociology. He did not attempt to provide an analysis
of what it is that may prevent justice, fairness and liberty from being
attained in particular societies in the contemporary world. He says, for
instance, that whether capitalism or socialism, or some mixture of the two

> most fully answers the requirements of justice cannot, I think, be
> determined in advance. There is presumably no general answer to
> this question, since it depends in large part upon the traditions,
> institutions, and social forces of each country, and its particular
> historical circumstances. The theory of justice does not include
> these matters.[3]

Rawls's work has been important as moral/political philosophy, but abstract if considered as social theory for it does not connect easily with the social practices in any existing society. Of course, it was not intended by Rawls that it should do so. For Gramsci, by contrast, philosophy should be concerned with heteronomy as well as with autonomy, that is with the limits placed on people's choices by their economic, political and cultural circumstances. As will be shown below sociology cannot be divorced from moral or political philosophy for Gramsci.

The work of another social theorist and social philosopher, Jurgen Habermas, is important in this context. Habermas has attempted to draw upon both German philosophy, including Kant and Hegel, and to use ideas drawn from linguistic philosophy. He too employs the Kantian distinction between heteronomy and autonomy as a basis for his social theory, the potential for rational autonomy being the distinguishing characteristic of human language users for Habermas. In addition, Hegel remains a significant background influence, if only because Habermas claims that Hegel produced the last 'system' of philosophy. Since Hegel, building grand philosophical systems has become impossible, as the Young Hegelians, but most crucially Marx, saw. Hegel had produced the last systematic 'idealist' philosophy, one in which Spirit (*Geist*), or consciousness, was ontologically fundamental. After Hegel, many philosophers, including Feuerbach for instance, turned to various forms of materialism in which the material basis of life attained more significance. Marx thought that this form of materialism was inadequate because it was too static and unconcerned with the role of human consciousness in economic and political change.

The methods of the sciences of nature came to exert a strong influence on the concerns of modern philosophers, including some Marxists. Crucially for later developments, Engels was influenced by this trend as will be discussed below. To such thinkers the natural sciences seemed to possess the only reliable way to attain real knowledge. Such an approach has since produced its own problems with which the philosophy of the social sciences still wrestles.

Habermas has tried to work consistently on this set of problems. He has suggested a shift of emphasis from the paradigm of material production, found in Marx, to the paradigm of communication as an addition to production, not as a replacement for it.[4]

Habermas's paradigm of communication is one in which the analytical model of 'the ideal speech situation' operates as a way of understanding, justifying and explaining, changes made in social practices towards a situation in which all participants are free to speak, and are able to communicate fully with others, with no fear of physical, economic, social or psychological pressures being brought to bear upon them to distort what they want to communicate. This enables Habermas to connect with themes in moral and political philosophy, such as the concern with justice, equality, and liberty. He has said for example:

> According to my conception, the philosopher ought to explain the moral point of view, and — as far as possible — justify the claim to universality of this explanation, showing why it does not merely reflect the moral intuitions of the average, male, middle-class member of modern Western society. Anything further than this is a matter for moral discourse between participants . . . In other words: the moral philosopher must leave the substantive questions which go beyond a fundamental critique of value-scepticism and value-relativism to the participants in moral discourse . . . .[5]

Habermas's viewpoint is important in so far as it tries to establish the logical viability of moral discourse. It is limited from the point of view taken here, as will become clearer in what follows, in that he eschews discussion, qua moral philosopher, of substantive moral issues.

To return to the major argument of this book. I am concerned to argue that, in trying to bridge the existing gap between the social sciences, sociology in particular, and moral/political philosophy, a concept such as that of hegemony is helpful if not essential. The work which Gramsci did on this concept forms a major link between philosophy and sociology. The link between the two subjects is made through Gramsci's concern with the issue of consent — that people should freely, autonomously and rationally understand and participate in the cultural, economic and political affairs of their society. This idea of free, rational, consent and participation has its roots in Aristotle's notion of a 'polis' and it is not surprising, therefore, to find similar ideas surfacing in other social and political philosophers' work. The concern Gramsci had with the issue of consent has similarities with the later work of both Habermas and Rawls. Indeed, following Gramsci we should be looking for links of this sort between social philosophies and social theories, not scorning a philosopher such as Habermas for being eclectic, as some have done.[6]

The Gramscian problematic of hegemony is concerned with which philosophy, or world-view, is fundamental in a society and, more specifically, which philosophy, if any , is to be found among the working classes in a capitalist social formation. Philosophy, in the Gramscian sense, is neither a purely academic discipline nor is it identical with what is termed 'ideology' in the Marxist tradition. Gramsci expressed his concerns in an important passage in the *Prison Notebooks* as follows:

It is essential to destroy the widespread prejudice that philosophy is a strange and difficult thing just because it is the specific intellectual activity of a particular category of specialists or of professional and systematic philosophers. It must first be shown that all men are 'philosophers', by defining the limits and characteristics of the 'spontaneous philosophy' which is proper to everybody. This philosophy is contained in:
1: language itself, which is a totality of determined notions and concepts and not just of words grammatically devoid of content; 2. 'common sense' and 'good sense'; 3. popular religion and, therefore, also in the entire system of beliefs, superstitions, opinions, ways of seeing things and of acting, which are collectively bundled together under the name of 'folklore'.[7]

It is important to note that Gramsci here makes the point, implicitly if not explicitly, that ordinary language contains philosophical notions within it which are not systematically organized but which nevertheless operate to affect perceptions and actions. Not only did Gramsci see the importance of paying attention to language for philosophy, no doubt as a consequence of his study of linguistics, literature and philosophy at Turin University, but also he saw the limitations of using so-called 'ordinary language' as a solution to philosophical problems in the manner of some styles of modern linguistic philosophy. This type of solution to the problems of philosophy is blocked in the Gramscian position because it holds, correctly in my view, that there are philosophical ideas contained within any ordinary language at any particular point in its development. If this is the case, then ordinary language cannot be used as a neutral court of appeal in which to settle philosophical disputes, for it will contain a bias towards certain solutions which are embedded within it. Examples of the presence of philosophical ideas in ordinary language can be found in conceptions about what constitutes personality, in moral ideas, in ideas about legal responsibility and in political ideas about duties of citizens to the state, for example.

Religion is also an important instance of the entry of philosophical, ethical, and metaphysical concepts and concerns into ordinary people's lives, alongside language itself. Gramsci thought that an important part of the work of the party 'will have to be devoted to the question of religion or world-view'.[8] this will be discussed in more detail in Chapter 4. For Gramsci, the Communist party must be and 'cannot but be the proclaimer and organizer of an intellectual and moral reform, which also means creating the terrain for a subsequent development of the national-popular collective will towards the realization of a superior, total form of modern civilization'.[9]

Although the state can affect this, other organizations are involved in determining which philosophy, if any, is widespread in a society, or in a whole area of the world, such as 'the English-speaking world'. Political parties which do not form the main government in a state may provide this kind of philosophical education. Universities, colleges, polytechnics and schools are involved in this process, and although most of them are funded in European societies by the state, or by the state allowing them to live on inherited wealth left to them by benefactors, nevertheless they do have a degree of autonomy from state interference with regard to matters of curricula and research. However, a state can interfere and may cut off funds for research in areas it decides either are not a priority or which are inimical to it. The state may try also to influence the curricula in schools, as well as those in universities and colleges.

The state and the major social institutions in civil society, such as religious organizations, do try to influence which philosophy is to be the hegemonic one in a society. In addition industrial organizations also influence the lives of their employees in ways which produce a set of beliefs, values and practices which are an incipient form of world outlook, or even philosophy, on Gramsci's view.[10]

Churches and religious organizations disseminate philosophical ideas and moral values, sometimes formulated at high levels of intellectual abstraction in their own teaching institutions. Such organizations need state permission to operate in civil society, something which may either be given formally, or exist as a matter of custom and practice. A state is able to control whether religious organizations raise monies, use endowmwnts, conduct ritual practices or organize their own education programmes; but once granted these freedoms, churches and religious movements may become important and effective sources of independent philosophy and of political criticism. They have provided a major source of philosophical education in the past, and continue to do so in the present, at varying levels of complexity. The educational process in which churches are involved is especially effective because it is linked with ritual activities, Gramsci argued. Churches have used audio-visual aids, music, painting and other arts, audience participation, and learning through active involvement, for centuries, long before these pedagogic methods became used in schools. The role churches have played, and still do play, as organizations which aid some groups, or classes, to achieve hegemony in a society, offered a model for Gramsci's own assumptions about the role of the Communist Party in trying to build up hegemony.

Some social scientists may well argue that this is hardly surprising — a modern political ideology such as Marxism is, so it is sometimes claimed, a functional equivalent to religion.[11] This is seen as a value-neutral point which may be made about the functions of ideologies being similar to, if not identical with, the sociological and psychological functions of a religion. Yet such a perspective derives from a philosophical form of positivism which gives no 'meaning' to propositions of the kind made in religious discourse because they are neither empirically verifiable, nor falsifiable, as are propositions which are part of the natural sciences or propositions in mathematics.

This principle of logical positivism, whether in its verificationist form, or in its falsifiability version, excludes religious and metaphysical propositions, moral judgements, political ideologies, and philosophy in the ordinary definition of the word, as used in the question: 'What is your philosophy of life?', as meaningful areas of discourse. Positivism, in its various guises, has long been the dominant epistemological position in the human and social sciences in spite of new positions having had some success from time to time, such as phenomenology, existentialism, structuralism and critical theory.

Positivism within the social sciences has sometimes led, quite consistently, to ethical and political relativism — for if there is strictly no 'meaning' in moral propositions then no specific value system may be said in any meaningful way to be worse or better than any other. No rational judgements can be made between political and moral systems according to any consistent version of positivism, because no meaning can be given to the judgements. Moral and political judgements may be seen by positivists as reports upon a speaker's feelings about an action. For example the claim that 'Torturing political prisoners is wrong' can be translated as 'I feel disgust at people being tortured for their political beliefs'. But such propositions cannot be seen as having any claims to objective rational criteria of morality for positivism.

An important, impressive, tightly argued, and influential version of logical positivism was produced by Wittgenstein, who wrote in his *Tractatus Logico-Philosophicus*:

> 6.41 The sense of the world must lie outside the world. In the world everything is as it is and happens as it does. In it there is no value — and if there were, it would be of no value . . .
> 6.42 . . . there can be no ethical propositions . . .
> 6.421 It is clear that ethics cannot be expressed. Ethics is transcendental.[12]

Positivistic social scientists have not moved on from this view, stated at the highest level of rigour by the early Wittgenstein. Later on Wittgenstein himself, however, rejected this viewpoint and came to a more relativist position by a different route, namely that of describing language games as the solution to philosophical problems. In his later book, *Philosophical Investigations*, he wrote:

> 124. Philosophy may in no way interfere with the actual use of language; it can in the end only describe it.
> For it cannot give it any foundation either.
> It leaves everything as it is . . . .[13]

The major problem with this second position is that it precisely leaves everything as it is. Ordinary language cannot be used as a final court of appeal to settle disputes in, or about, philosophy because it itself contains ideas derived from philosophy; it is not some neutral territory immune to philosophical concepts which it would need to be if the later Wittgensteinian position was to be a satisfactory solution to the problems of philosophy. This means that concepts which have entered ordinary language from earlier world views — concepts such as 'sin', or 'individual responsibility', or 'duty' — permeate discourse. Ordinary language has been infused with philosophical terms and ideas in the past which have left traces in the language various groups use in the present.

Wittgenstein's injunction for philosophy to leave language as it is came too late; language had been interfered with already. Philosophy could purport to rid ordinary language of past philosophical ideas, thereby reducing muddle and confusion, but what would be left as ordinary language could not be used to perform some central social practices in law, politics, education, in families, in religions, or in work situations.

Wittgenstein's notion of philosophy as consisting of the description of language games, and showing them as rule-governed social activities, leaves all of them as ongoing social practices. If philosophers became critical of some of these language games the question would arise of the standpoint from which such criticism was being conducted and of whether some one standpoint could be more justified than another. The bases for establishing such a standpoint would then form the major activity of philosophy — again. Philosophy in this sense will not die.

The problematic which began with the development of the concept of hegemony is important in this context because it raises both the question of which philosophical viewpoint should be hegemonic, or leading and directive, in a society — in the economy, in the state and in civil society. The first problem is one within philosophy and politics; the second is one in what could be called 'the sociology of philosophy'. They are interrelated because the sociology used for answering the second question derives its epistemological base from the philosophy chosen in answering the first problem. The choice of a philosophy, or method of doing philosophy, is in part a political and moral choice. Such a moral and political choice has an intellectual component to it; it is not only based on emotions but on reasons too.

Hegemony, in its most complete form, is defined as occurring when the intellectual, moral and philosophical leadership provided by the class or alliance of classes and class fractions which is ruling, successfully achieves its objective of providing the fundamental outlook for the whole society. Ruling groups also have the coercive apparatus of the state, that is the police and armed forces, at their disposal; in this sense they are said to be 'dominant' too in Gramscian terminology. They may also be powerful in the economic area as owners of substantial industrial or commercial property; or they may be career politicians with no substantial amounts of such property of their own; in either case they are said to rule hegemonically if, and only if, they pursue policies which are not in the direct, narrow, interst of capitalists, but rather which can be presented plausibly as being in the interests of the whole people, of the nation. As C. Buci-Glucksmann put it:

> The more authentically hegemonic a class really is, the more it leaves opposing classes the possibility of organizing and forming themselves into an autonomous political force. [14]

Under modern capitalist conditions the activities of socialists in the economic sphere tend to be limited to trade unionism, that is to the economic-corporate defence of the material interests of workers. For Gramsci this is not the same thing as establishing hegemonic leadership. In such conditions, Gramsci argued, that:

> it is necessary to begin . . . from a study of the doctrine which belongs to the working class, which is the philosophy of the working class, which is the sociology of the working class: from a study of historical materialism, from a study of Marxism.[15]

This marks a call for a 'new intellectualism', particularly for philosophical activity, among the masses, as "a liberating dimension of the masses' political autonomy".[16]

The choice of a philosophical position was made, in Gramsci's case, on the basis of a desire to produce a different political and economic system from that of capitalism, in Italy and in the world at large. The reasons for this desire for change were moral ones — for without such a change the masses would continue to remain undeveloped, not realizing their potential as human beings and remaining subject to economic crises and to wars. Gramsci thought that for peace to exist a change in the world's capitalist structures was necessary if conflicts between the European powers were to be avoided.

It is difficult to see how this choice can be characterized as being anything other than a moral-political one in the first instance. Such a choice cannot be construed as one which results from simply recognizing what is produced by the 'science' of Marxism without a collapse into a form of positivism — a positivism which holds that science will provide such guidance as the species requires about how the world is to be orgnized and ordered. This particular form of positivism may be termed 'scientism'. Scientism holds that there are no meaningful forms of discourse other than those of science, and this has to include the social sciences if it is to generate policies for a society to follow. Philosophy is ruled out as meaningless; political philosophy and morality are non-rational, meaningless discourses.

Scientism may lead to theoretical 'anti-humanism', in the sense of treating the concept 'human' as being outside of any scientific discourse and incapable of being treated as a theoretically constituted scientific 'object'. Unless some other form of discourse, such as moral philosophy, is allowed as constituting a meaningful discourse, which is something scientism cannot consistently allow, then this philosophical position does produce, logically, a form of theoretical anti-humanism.

The choice of a philosophical standpoint is a moral choice in that a person begins from a position in which human beings are seen as either having moral capacities, or from a view that they are determined and, like other creatures, have no moral or rational autonomy, potentially or in fact. If human beings are not fully determined, but potentially can think rationally and act autonomously, then this entails that moral philosophy is a possible intellectual activity. Moral philosophy then has the task of providing a justification for these claims of the possibility of rational, free, autonomous decisions and actions, and of countering relativism, determinism, and value-scepticism. These are value claims in any case, so unlike Habermas's view of this matter, mentioned above, it seems that this activity of moral philosophy cannot easily be distinguished from that of making value judgements of a substantive type.[17]

Once it has been established that moral philosophy is possible, then it is necessary to analyse the processes involved in preventing people being able to exercise moral choice. To do this it is necessary to move into social theory. Social theory here means a theory which can conceptualize what it is in particular historical situations which prevents the realization of the moral, rational, free, and autonomous choices people are potentially capable of making. These social theoretical concepts then have to be applied to concrete situations, in particular societies, in specific studies in the various social sciences.

The problematic of hegemony is not merely a concept about the social position of philosophies in societies. It also claims to be a central part of a specific moral/political philosophy, or world-view, that of 'the philosophy of praxis'. The concept of hegemony is not only a social theoretical, analytical concept, therefore, but it is also part of a moral philosophical viewpoint. The meaning of this statement will be explored further in the next section of this chapter.

PHILOSOPHY AND SOCIAL THEORY IN MARX

So far in this chapter, I have examined the relationship between philosophy, especially moral and political philosophy, and the social sciences, on the basis of a criticism of positivist epistemology implied in the problematic of hegemony. In this section the development of the relations between philosophy and social theory is explored within Marxism more specifically, before further analysis of hegemony in the final section of this chapter.

Marx had developed his work out of a critique of three main bodies of writings, namely German Hegelian philosophy, the political economy of Adam Smith and Ricardo, and the political ideas in the work of Proudhon. Out of his criticism of these writers he developed his own position which can be seen as a contribution to both European philosophy and as a contribution to social theory, sociology and political economy. There are, therefore, two major aspects in Marx's works, namely the social scientific and the philosophical, which has produced a debate about whether these represent two distinct kinds of theory in Marx or only one.

The view that there are two Marxes, a young Marx and a 'mature' Marx, is sometimes put in terms of the work of the younger Marx having been more philosophical, and that of the later Marx on political economy, and on the social theory of modes of production, as having been more scientific. Althusser, for example, stressed the 'epistemological break', as he called it, between the early, unscientific work of Marx, and the later work which founded a new science for the analysis of modes of production, the exact position and date of the split between the two Marxes varying in Althusser's own different phases of writing.[18] Others, who also hold that it is useful to think in terms of there having been two quite different types of work in Marx, hold that philosophy is present in some parts of the later works as it is in the early texts, but that nevertheless these two types of writings, the philosophical and the scientific, both have value. The Italian Marxist, Lucio Colletti, for example, writing in the nineteen-seventies, tended towards this view.

Colletti argued that any discourse which can be called a 'science' can only deal with realities which contain real oppositions, conflicts between forces, and not with dialectical contradictions: '. . . capitalist contradictions are, for Marx, dialectical contradictions and not real oppositions'.[19] For Colletti dialectical contradictions cannot be approached scientifically, but must be approached philosophically. Therefore, it follows, that Marx's analysis of capitalism was philosophical, not scientific. However, Colletti also argued that:

> science is the only means of apprehending reality, the only means of gaining knowledge about the world. Furthermore, there cannot be two (qualitatively different) forms of knowledge. A philosophy which claims a status for itself superior to that of science, is an edifying philosophy- that is, a scarcely disguised religion.[20]

Colletti concluded that there were:

> two aspects in Marx: that of the scientist and that of the philosopher . . . The social sciences have not yet found a true foundation of their own. Hence I do not know whether the existence of these two aspects is fatal or advantageous. What is not at issue is the fact that our task now is to find out whether and how they can be reconciled.[21]

The main problem with this argument lies in the assumption that there cannot be two forms of knowledge which are qualitatively different: philosophy and science. If one assumes that the methods of the natural sciences are not applicable to the social and human sciences because human actions, as distinct from behaviour patterns, are not fully determined but can potentially be autonomous and rational, then Colletti's assumption can be rejected. Philosophy, in particular moral and political philosophy, would then be seen to impinge upon, and overlap with, the human and social sciences because these human sciences logically involve assumptions having to be made about moral and political values.

There are indeed two qualitatively different forms of knowledge, those of the natural sciences and those produced by philosophical reasoning, messy though this assumption may seem to some. Some things which happen to human beings, as in the realm of disease for instance, and some physical characteristics which a human body possesses such as skin, hair and eye colour, can be seen as caused, or as determined, by physiological, genetic, biochemical, neurological, and other biological factors. But such occurrences are not then describable as 'human actions', but as caused happenings or events. The distinction between the two tyes of discourse is fundamental. The human, or social, sciences describe and try to explain human actions and their unintended consequences. Such unintended consequences are not things which happen to us as a result of natural processes but are the result of social, historical processes. The discourses of the human sciences overlap, therefore, with moral and political philosophy as a matter of logic. The implications of this assertion will be explored below. First, there is another view of the work of Marx which must be mentioned at this point.

The view that there is really only one Marx, that the same theme, or themes, runs through all his work, and that this is a contribution to social theory conceived of as a blend of social science and philosophy, has been argued by some. I. Meszaros (1970), for example, following the earlier work of Lukacs and Lenin, stressed that the concepts of alienation, estrangement, reification, and fetishism, were a related set of constant concerns in all of Marx's works. For instance he argued:

> As Lenin had brilliantly perceived, the central idea of Marx's system is his critique of the capitalistic reification of the social relations of production, the alienation of labour through the reified mediations of wage labour, private property, and exchange.[22]

Meszaros treats Marx's thought as being of a new type, neither Hegelian philosophy, nor positivistic economic science, nor a kind of natural science of history. The latter would be a contradiction in any case because historical events are not to be seen as causally determined as events in nature are said to be 'caused' for this would omit the capacity of human beings to act in history. Marx produced a social theory which was linked rigorously with a philosophy about human beings' potentialities, on this view of his works.

D. McLellan (1971) has taken a related view, emphasizing the central link provided by the *Grundrisse* (1857–58) between the early works, especially on alienation, in the *Paris Manuscripts* of 1844, and the later analysis in *Capital* (1867). McLellan stated, for instance, that:

> the term 'alienation', which occurs much more in *Capital* than some writers appear to think, . . . is central to most of the more important passges of the *Grundrisse*.[23]

There is also a view, found in many Marxist political groups, that Marx produced a new way of operating which combined theory and practice and at the same time dispensed with the separate academic discipline boundaries of bourgeois thought — the boundaries between philosophy, economics, history, sociology, and politics. It does not matter, therefore, whether Marx is seen as a philosopher or as a scientist for he displaced both as separate ways of working in the field of the human and social sciences. The thrust of Marx's break with academic, bourgeois, disciplines was made in his much-quoted eleventh thesis on Feuerbach:

> The philosophers have only interpreted the world in different ways; the point is to change it.[24]

This perspective, held by some activists, can become so oriented to practical affairs that Marx's aim of realizing in history the goals and values of his philosophy is lost in a form of empiricism and pragmatism.

A major problem in many of the contributions to the debate about what Marx achieved is the positivist definition of philosophy which operates within them, as illustrated even by Colletti's position. The positive evaluation of science as a mode of thinking superior to all others, indeed displacing other modes of thought, also seems to haunt Althusser's work in some respects. (Meszaros and McLellan, however, do avoid the positivistic trap.) Philosophy is seen by positivists as being incapable of yielding 'scientific' knowledge about the social or natural worlds. Philosophy is seen as a problem discipline, even as a meaningless one, because it does not produce scientific knowledge about the natural or the social worlds. It becomes, therefore, very difficult both to acknowledge that Marx wrote in a philosophical vein and, at the same time, to preserve his status as the founder of the science of society, of history, or of modes of production.

The view that philosophy might have a legitimate place as a discipline concerned with epistemological issues; that philosophy could establish that there are other important types of rationally grounded discourse than those of 'science'; and that in particular rational debates about moral and political value judgements are possible; is one which is dismissed by many influenced by positivism. Colletti, for example, uses the phrases 'an edifying philosophy' and 'disguised religion' to describe, and at the same time to ridicule, such a position.[25] He makes no allowance for rationally grounded moral and political discourse; propositions are either 'scientific' or 'religious' (edifying philosophy). This is positivistic in the sense that it treats science as being the only source of meaningful knowledge about the social as well as the natural world. Ethics as a branch of philosophy becomes meaningless, or 'merely religious'. This position fails to acknowledge precisely the most important area of discourse to which Marxism has contributed — that of a rationally grounded political and moral philosophy linked with a social theory about the workings of capitalism and how it might be changed or overcome.[26]

Gramsci saw Marxism as a philosophy in both the technical, academic sense and in the more everyday sense of the term. He thought that philosophy at the academic level would include both epistemology and ethics as two central components, but that philosophy is also 'a conception of the world', one which is more coherently organized than common sense itself.

Some positivistic communist leaders and writers, in the Soviet Union and elsewhere, have sought to turn Marxism into a science and to cut it off from philosophy. If Marxism is to count as a real contribution to knowledge it must be a science, it is held, because only sciences produce knowledge. On the other hand Marxism appears to many Western positivists like no other science because some of its propositions are irrefutable they would argue. For example, the claim, 'The history of all hitherto existing societies is the history of class struggles', may look like an empirically testable proposition but in fact no evidence is ever allowed to count against it by communists; it operates more like a religious dogma than a scientific proposition non-Marxist positivists claim.

It is necessary to make an epistemological break with both these forms of positivism and to treat political/moral philosophy more seriously. Moral and political philosophy can constitute a rational discourse, aiming to clarify the basic concepts of political and moral discussion among human agents.

Gramsci had emphasized that it was politics which linked the academic level of philosophy with the 'good sense' conception of philosophy as a coherently organized world-view.[27] Politics was defined by Gramsci very widely, so as to include all major aspects of social life. For Gramsci it was a philosophy, not a science, which could become hegemonic in a society. There would be something nonsensical about the idea of a science being hegemonic. It was part of the definition of hegemony that it involved intellectual, moral and philosophical leadership; such leadership was not seen as being the technical application of a science.

This notion of philosophy is not the same as 'ideology' for Gramscian theory, because the term 'ideology' carries the connotation of either something which is untrue, or false, or which disguises other, material, interests within itself. Philosophy is not false, or untrue, nor is it a disguise for other material interests, but has its own rational and autonomous realm of discourse.

It is also not possible to speak of a 'science' being hegemonic because sciences as such do not provide moral and political judgements, without which ruling is impossible, on Gramsci's view. Ruling is not describable as an activity consisting of the application of a science; it involves both the exercise of coercive power and the production of hegemonic consent to policies which necessitate choices between competing values — choices such as incresing wealth by allowing some increase in inequalities in material rewards, or emphasizing equality as the foremost value; or of allowing, or not allowing, the expression of dissent about perceived injustices in a state. Ruling is an activity based upon making moral and political judgements.

MORAL-POLITICAL PHILOSOPHY AND HEGEMONY

So far in this chapter we have seen that the problematic of hegemony involves two components: one component is a moral-political philosophy, which is linked with the second, a social theory about modern societies. It has been argued that each component is necessary to the other if intellectual confusion is to be avoided. Ethics without sociology and social theory is abstract; social theory not based upon explicit moral and political values is confused and confusing.

The second component, the social theory, as discussed here is primarily concerned with Western European capitalist societies, but an important comparison between these societies and the Soviet Union, in the first two decades after the 1917 Revolution, was made by Gramsci in the process of developing the concept of hegemony.

Moral-political philosophy is the area of philosophy which is concerned with the analysis of those moral concepts which have a political dimension to them; concepts such as justice, liberty, freedom, equality, democracy, and peace, together with their opposites. Both the relationships between, and the priorities among, these values are a central concern of moral-political philosophy, as was illustrated by the work of Rawls and Habermas mentioned above. These issues in moral-political philosophy cannot easily be dodged by dismissing them as being 'utopian', not 'scientific', as some dogmatic, economistic Marxists might be tempted to do.

Nevertheless, moral-political philosophy can appear utopian, that is cut off from concrete circumstances, if the philosophical aspect is left without any systematic connection with a social theory. It was suggested in the first section of this chapter that there was some danger that the work of Rawls could appear to be utopian in that it was too cut off from concrete social theory, for example. The notion of 'social theory' in this context includes those aspects of sociology and political economy which conceptualize concrete situations in such a way that it is possible to assess what can be changed in a specific social situation towards the realization of one or more moral-political values.[28] Gramsci's problematic of hegemony began to develop both aspects, the philosophical and the social theoretical, developing these from the work of Marx.[29]

Marx's own work may be seen as having contained a moral-political philosophical position, as well as a social theory about capitalism in particular. In the *Critique of the Gotha Programme* (1875), for instance, Marx analysed the connection between certain values, in this case the notion of fairness in distribution, and the limitations the prevailing economic circumstances of the capitalist mode of production placed upon the notion of fairness being realized in the distribution of the social product.

Even after a revolution in the mode of production, during the first phase of communism, Marx argued, the consumption of goods would depend upon the time spent in labouring activities, in spite of the differences between people in the amount of labour they supplied in the same time, or the length of time they were able to labour as a result of the fact that: 'one man is superior to another physically or mentally . . .'.[30]
Marx went on to conclude that:

> Right can never be higher than the economic structure of society
> and its cultural development conditioned thereby.

In a second, higher phase of communist society, when primary needs have been met and 'the antithesis between mental and physical labour has vanished', then and only then can society operate on the basis of the principle: 'From each according to his ability, to each according to his needs!'[31]

This text combined a social theoretical analysis of what is possible in specific circumstances of a society, linked with moral-political philosophical principles, although the arguments for these principles are not presented in this particular context. However, it did suggest that moral political philosophy had to be conducted within the context of a social theory about 'the economic structure of society and its cultural development conditioned thereby'. Moral philosophy conducted outside such a social theoretical context runs the danger of being merely utopian.

In the work of Gramsci there was a similar set of links established between the social theory of concrete societies and moral political philosophy as those found in Marx. The problematic of hegemony aimed to show that some of the moral and intellectual developments which communisim required, if it was to obtain people's active consent, could start to be produced within the bosom of capitalism. This too had been a major point Marx made — that a new society starts to develop in the womb of the old. Of course there was a major difference between the circumstances of Marx and Gramsci in that Gramsci could refer to 'actually existing socialism' in the Soviet Union, from which experience could be gained. Indeed it was the way in which the Russian Revolution had developed which suggested to Gramsci the need to develop hegemonic leadership among the people, especially in Western Europe, before any assault upon the coercive state apparatus was possible. If this was not done a revolution would become experienced as an imposition upon ordinary people, made by a small elite, even if it could succeed in the first place.

One further point should be mentioned in this context. This is that although Gramsci used and commented upon the work of Machiavelli in the *Prison Notebooks*, he was not 'Machiavellian' in the way that term is used in modern English. To call Gramsci's approach 'Machiavellian' would distort completely the meaning of seeking to build up hegemonic moral and intellectual leadership. For the active consent of people which Gramsci sought for the philosophy of praxis cannot be produced as a result of any kind of machinations among a state's politicians, nor by the manipulation of the people by revolutionary parties or sects.

Within 'orthodox' versions of communism, as mentioned above, the emphasis has been upon the economic theory in Marxism rather than the moral-political philosophy. Marxist economic theory has been considered to be a scientific theory in either the positivistic and historist sense, as a set of value-free propositions about what will happen in world-history, or even as stating the laws governing history, or in a structuralist sense as in the case of Althusser. In the latter case, Marx is presented as having developed a new science, concerned with the theoretically constructed object 'modes of production', capitalism in particular, but precisely not about human beings' possibilities and potentialities being realized in history. Althusser sought to eradicate these humanist elements in his reading of Marx.[32]

At this point it is useful to examine Engels's text *Socialism: Utopian and Scientific* of 1892.[33] The issues raised in this text of Engels remain in the contemporary situation, albeit in slightly altered form, as may be seen in the disputes which have arisen between 'scientific' Marxists, whether structuralist or positivist, and those who might be called philosophical Marxists. It can seem, at first sight, that traditonal Marxism, as presented by Engels, would support the scientific form and would reject the more philosophical versions of Marxism as being forms of utopianism.

Engels argued that Marx had created a science of socialism which explained, in a way earlier utopian socialism had not been able to do, that the exploitation of the workers was inevitable under capitalism.[34] If this was so there was little point in saying that such exploitation was morally wrong, for this would be equivalent to saying that an earthquake which killed hundreds of people was morally wrong. Just as an earthquake is not a moral agent neither, on this view is a mode of production. Moral categories are inapplicable to such entities on this view.

Marx had shown the inevitability of capitalism under certain historical conditions, Engels claimed, together with its equally inevitable downfall as a result of its own internal contradictions between the mode of production, which was socially organised, and the mode of exchange which was individualised. Crises developed as a result of over-production, unsold goods, and the unemployment which ensued. Engels wrote:

> The contradiction has grown into an absurdity. The mode of production rises in rebellion against the form of exchange.[35]

Marx had also conceptualized the essential character of modern capitalism, which lay in the idea that capitalism extracted 'surplus value' from labour.[36] Scientific socialism, as distinct from the utopian socialism of the social philosophers, recognizes that it is not enough to point out that capitalist exploitation is immoral and unjust. It is necessary to show that historical conditions affect what is possible. Engels wrote:

> the final causes of all social changes and political revolutions are to be sought, not in men's brains, not in men's better insight into eternal truth and justice, but in changes in the modes of production and exchange. They are to be sought, not in the philosophy, but in the economics of each particular epoch. The growing perception that existing social institutions are unreasonable and unjust, that reason has become unreason and right wrong, is only proof that in the modes of production and exchange changes have silently taken place with which the social order, adapted to earlier economic conditions, is no longer in keeping.[37]

This passage may be understood as entailing the conclusion that philosophy is no longer necessary. Indeed, earlier on in the same text Engels had argued that philosophy was no longer needed, except as formal logic and dialectics. 'Everything else is subsumed in the positive science of Nature and history.'[38]

However, if one asks the standard philosophical questions about such statements concerning the 'end of philosophy' — namely, What kind of proposition is the proposition about the end of philosophy itself considered to be? Are the arguments that lead to it to be seen as being a part of science, or of formal logic, or of dialectics? — then problems arise. For such propositions about the end, or impossibility, of philosophy are not part of any science; nor do they appear as propositions within formal logic, nor within dialectics. Engels's own text, therefore, is itself difficult to place within the categories of thought which he accepts as being possible. It is a mixture of philosophical, epistemological, arguments and propositions, and some propositions within social theory about social change and the nature of capitalism. Engel's text contains both philosophical proposals about science and moral-political judgements, together with the claim that philosophy is redundant. In other words, it is inconsistent.

Engels judged moves and arguments within moral-political philosophy, produced by those he called 'utopian socialists' (Fourier, Saint-Simon, and Owen) by rules derived from his dialectical understanding of some natural sciences, such as Darwinian biology.[39] There is no necessity, however, to choose between sciences and moral-political philosophy, as Engels suggested there is. Both are necessary for different purposes. But it is illegitimate, logically, to prefer one type of discourse alone, and to judge all others by this preferred type, which for positivists is natural scientific discourse. Engels was guilty of doing just this — taking natural science as the measure of all other types of discourse.

Engels tried to persuade the reader by reasoned arguments that capitalism was doomed to disappear and that it would be replaced by socialism. However, it is not clear whether the arrival of socialism/communism was seen as being inevitable and that it would arrive automatically, or whether people would need to be persuaded to act in ways which would help to bring it about. The latter seems to be a part of what the text is trying to achieve. It ends by calling for the proletariat 'to accomplish this act of universal emancipation', i.e. revolution.[40] To do this requires, however, the theoretical side of the proletarian movement to introduce to the 'oppressed proletarian class a full knowledge of the conditions and of the meaning of the momentous task it is called upon to accomplish . . .'.[41] The text both attempts to argue that the collapse of capitalism from internal contradictions, and the arrival of socialism, is inevitable, and that people should act in ways which will help bring it about. Engels wrote:

> Active social forces work exactly like natural forces: blindly, forcibly, destructively, so long as we do not understand, and reckon with, them. But when once we understand them, when once we grasp their action, their direction, their effects, it depends only upon ourselves to subject them more and more to our will, and by means of them to reach our own ends.[42]

Gramsci argued more explicitly than Engels that rational, moral, philosophical and emotional arguments may be needed to motivate people to try to achieve socialism/communism, as a 'better', or higher, social formation than capitalism. It is not inevitable that capitalism will be replaced by socialism; barbarism was the alternative mentioned by Marx and to some extent witnessed by Gramsci in his lifetime.

The importance of Gramsci's problematic of hegemony was that it broke with conceptions of Marxism as a positivistic science of the kind which Engels's text all too easily suggested — whether seen as a science based upon the inevitable laws of economics, or as a science based on the discovery of the laws governing history, as though Marx had been the Darwin of the science of history. In place of these understandings of Marx, Gramsci considered it was necessary to present his work as 'the philosophy of praxis', using this term not just as a disguise to avoid the prison censor, but as a serious contribution to a proper understanding of Marxism as a political philosophy allied with a social theory and a political practice.

Although structuralist conceptions of science had not emerged in Gramsci's lifetime, the central emphases in his work do imply a critique of structuralist versions of Marxism which claim that Marxism should be seen as primarily a science, divorced from the humanism and from the moral-political philosophy in Marx's own work. For Gramsci raised issues concerned with the notion of human agency, will, and moral philosophy within a framework of a social theory which could both explain why certain values were hegemonic and others were not, and could guide intellectual and political praxis (that is theoretically informed political practice). These humanistic and moral philosophical aspects of Gramsci's thought were rejected, or ignored, by Althusser, for instance, even though he held that Gramsci had made real advances in Marxism, especially with the concepts of hegemony and coercive power in the state.

Gramsci's theory was not based upon the same epistemological position as Althusser's. Althusser emphasized science as the basis of knowledge, science understood as having theoretically conceived objects of analysis, not as based upon theory-free empirical observations; but he rejected anything to do with moral philosophy, which he saw as being 'ideology' not 'science'. On the other hand Gramsci's philosophical base — the philosophy of praxis — was taken from Marx, he claimed.

'Praxis' was too humanistic a concept for Althusser. Praxis refers to human action conducted upon a theoretically produced viewpoint. The notion of human action was rejected by Althusser for being unscientific. Furthermore, the concept of human action as praxis was too Hegelian for Althusser. Praxis was an idealist conception because it was involved with subjectivist views of human consciousness in Althusser's view. Such a humanistic conception as that of 'praxis' fails to grasp that subjects are constituted by structures, or by discourses, in the view of both Althusserians and later post-structuralists.

In the criticisms which have developed of Althusser, however, a key theme has been the absence in his theory of an adequate conception of agency in producing change. It was in this context that a return to Gramsci became necessary.[43] Gramsci had emphasized the importance of agency, of moral and intellectual leadership. This was linked with a new social theory about modern European, capitalist societies, and a strategy for achieving change in them, as can be seen in Gramsci's analysis of 'a war of position' in Western European societies, which was discussed in Chapter 1. It can be said, in a way which is compatible with the Gramscian problematic, that without a social theory any moral-political philosophy becomes merely abstract, removed from actual or potential influence in concrete political, socio-cultural and economic structures. So moral philosophy requires systematic links to be made with a social theory if it is to avoid being ineffective.

Equally, however, it may be said in a way which is compatible with Gramsci's position, that social, political and economic theories require to be grounded in, and systematically linked with, moral-political philosophy, otherwise they run the risk of forming the basis for non-democratic ideologies which may falsely call themselves 'sciences'. Such ideologies may become experienced as external impositions upon people, especially by those subjected to them in political practice. The Gramscian notion of hegemonic leadership requires that millions of ordinary people come to accept, in the sense of really giving their free consent to, the political, economic and cultural policies being pursued by the dominant ruling group. This means that a political programme based upon a political-economic social theory must be actively related to the moral values people understand and hold. If this is not done, people may well feel manipulated into having to tolerate particular policies pursued by ruling groups, or dominated and ruled against their consent, a situation which can lead to the use of violent coercion by the state.

Hegemony, when successfully achieved, is unnoticeable in everyday political, cultural and economic life. If, however, change is desired by some groups who are not dominant either in the state, or in the economy, then they will need to engage in a hegemonic struggle. Such was the situation of socialists in West European capitalism on Gramsci's view. This struggle for hegemony will take the form initially of moral and philosophical argument in the media and in education, not primarily in the form of direct actions nor in actions of a narrow economic-corporate kind. These latter types of action often become institutionalized, being defined by the leading groups as the activities of deviant minorities, whose rights to protest peacefully must be protected in Western democracies. Such institutionalized activities have little chance of achieving changes of the system. Alternatively, in a situation of weak hegemony for the dominant groups, the police, and even the army, may be used to take action against the perpetrators of protest actions and strikes. Unless the situation has become a revolutionary one, the dominant group in the state, and/or in the economy, will win these battles.

Hegemonic struggle in a Gramscian 'war of position' must precede, therefore, any direct assault on the state's coercive structures. In Gramsci's view, the situation in Western Europe was quite distinct from that during the First World War in Tsarist Russia, where a war of movement had been possible. Western European conditions necessitated a different strategy. Gramsci argued that:

> In Russia the state was everything, civil society was primordial and gelatinous; in the West, there was a proper relation between state and civil society, and when the state trembled a sturdy structure of civil society was at once revealed. The state was only an outer ditch, behind which there stood a powerful system of fortresses and earthworks: more or less numerous from one state to the next it goes without saying — but this precisely necessitated an accurate reconnaisance of each individual country. [44]

In spite of all the military analogies in Gramsci's writing, the struggle for hegemony is moral, intellectual and philosophical in his analysis. Some components of the hegemonic struggle would take place in political parties, which are included in the analytical category of civil society — unless a party is in power and in charge of the state's coercive system. When organizing and competing for votes parties are seen as being part of civil society. Hegemonic struggle may take place also in voluntary orgnizations, religious organizations, pressure groups, trades unions, and in the educational system. Some of the work has to be done at the highest intellectual level in philosophy and the social sciences. Other parts of the work are oriented to teaching students of all ages. As was pointed out in Chapter 1 there is also a need for politicians and other public figures to communicate with ordinary people in a nation at a more emotional level — a feature stressed by Gramsci partly because he saw both the emotional appeal to some of the masses of Catholicism, of Italian fascism and nationalist political ideologies of the right.[45]

Only in this way can a 'historical bloc' be created which can effect change, in Gramsci's view. This would entail links being made between the class which is in hegemonic leadership in civil society and that which leads in the economic sphere of production. The bourgeoisie had achieved this in Britain and France, but not in Italy; the proletariat would need to form such a historic bloc for any major change in Western Europe. A system of alliances with other groups, such as that between peasants and industrial workers in Italy, was also part of the Gramscian strategy. As was discussed above, Lenin had argued in his early pamphlet, *What is to be done?* (1902), before the later assault on the state in a war of manoeuvre, that alliances between all groups wanting change in Tsarist Russia was necessary, including the petit bourgeoisie, teachers, rural peasants and the urban, industrial workers. This aspect of Lenin's praxis was developed by Gramsci for the situation in Western Europe in the nineteen-thirties, and by the Italian Communist Party since the end of the Second World War. The war of manoeuvre was not possible in highly developed Western Europe; capturing the state, even if this were possible, would not necessarily produce the changes sought in civil society. So Gramsci developed a different strategy which could be thought by some to be 'un-Marxist' because it had elements in it which seemed to be a revival of what Engels had called utopian, as distinct from scientific, socialism.

There is a role in the Gramscian perspective for intellectual work in building up a new hegemonic group in civil society. It is important, for instance, to establish that moral-political philosophy is epistemologically viable. This is not something which Gramsci himself did, although he provided some critical, philosophical commentary upon Croce, Gentile, and Kant, for instance.[46] However, it was pointed out in the first section of this chapter that Habermas has tried to establish that moral philosophy is possible, as against the various forms of relativism, scientism, and positivism which deny that it is a logically viable form of discourse.

Gramsci termed Marxism, as was mentioned above, 'the philosophy of praxis'. This is a form of moral-political philosophy integrated with a social theory. It does not present Marxism primarily as a scientific theory of economic modes of production as Althusser attempted to do. In order to develop the philosophy of praxis as the hegemonic philosophy in civil society in the first instance, it is necessary to return to fundamental epistemological issues. The term 'philosophy of praxis', which Gramsci used, connotes a fundamental aspect of his approach to Marxism as a philosophy which was neither a crude form of materialism, positivism, determinism nor historicism. The philosophy of praxis is:

> a 'materialism' perfected by the work of speculative philosophy itself and fused with humanism.[47]

Each of the terms in the above quotation is important here. The philosophy of praxis combines materialism, in that it conceptualizes the material production of life through labour, with a conceptualization derived from Hegelian idealism, or speculative philosophy, of the cultural and intellectual life of historical epochs. The relationship between these two is not conceived of as being such that one, the material, the economic, determined the other, the realm of culture and ideologies. Rather Gramsci sees the relationship between the material, productive base, and the cultural sphere as being a complex, reciprocal one in which human beings mediate between the two zones. Hence the philosophy of praxis is a humanism. Human beings, and their economic, political and cultural conditions, are a central concern. They are what the philosophy of praxis is fundamentally about for Gramsci as for Marx on this interpretation.

The concept of 'praxis' itself connotes nor merely practice, as in crude versions of pragmatism or historicism where what is true, or theoretically acceptable, is judged purely on the basis of what enables certain posited results of action to be obtained, including a particular political party to obtain power, but also theoretically conceived practices.[48] The philosophy of praxis provides a philosophy, a view of human beings and their needs, desires, and requirements, based upon realistic scientific knowledge about man as a species, together with the philosophical notion that men and women are potentially creative and socially cooperative rather than mutually antagonistic. Such a moral philosophy, allied with a social theory, could specify what needs to be done, and what it is possible to do, in a given society to change it in a direction which would help to realize these potentialities.

The relationship between the economic and the cultural sphere, which includes major religious systems, is not a deterministic one for Gramsci. His work has some parallels at this point with that of the sociologist Max Weber. These similarities between Gramsci and Weber, as well as the differences between them, will be discussed in the next chapter.

REFERENCES

[1] The 'tradition' of separating facts and values is often seen to stem from David Hume, but this was challenged by A. MacIntyre in *A Short History of Ethics*, London, Routledge & Kegan Paul, 1967, Chapter 12. A major example of an influential work in moral, political philosophy is J. Rawls, *A Theory of Justice*, Harvard, 1971; Oxford University Press, 1978.

[2] J. Rawls, op. cit., 1978 edition, pp. 251–252.

[3] Ibid., p. 274.

[4] J. Habermas, *Knowledge and Human Interests*, translated by J.

Shapiro, London, Heinemann, 1972. J. Habermas, *Theory and Practice*, translated by J. Viertel, London, Heinemann, 1974. And interview with Habermas in *New Left Review*, No. 151, 1985, p. 96.

[5] *New Left Review*, No. 151, 1985, p. 84.

[6] See G. Therborn, 'Jurgen Habermas: A New Eclecticism', *New Left Review*, No. 67, 1971, pp. 69–83.

[7] A. Gramsci, *Selections from the Prison Notebooks*, edited and translated by Q. Hoare & G. Nowell Smith, London, Lawrence & Wishart, 1971 (=SPN), p. 323.

[8] SPN, p. 132.

[9] SPN, p. 133.

[10] SPN, 'Americanism and Fordism', pp. 279–318.

[11] See M. Yinger, *The Scientific Study of Religion*, Macmillan, New York, 1970, 'Religious Aspects of Marxism', pp. 196–200.

[12] L. Wittgenstein, *Tractatus Logico-Philosophicus,* first published 1922; London, Routledge & Kegan Paul, 1960.

[13] L. Wittgenstein, *Philosophical Investigations*, Oxford, Blackwell, 1953. Peter Winch used this later Wittgensteinian position in his book *The Idea of a Social Science*, London, Routledge & Kegan Paul, 1958.

[14] C. Buci-Glucksmann, *Gramsci and the State*, London, Lawrence & Wishart, 1980, p. 57.

[15] A. Gramsci, *Political Writings, 1921–1926*, London, Lawrence and Wishart, p. 171.

[16] C. Buci-Glucksmann, op. cit., p. 336.

[17] See J. Habermas, *New Left Review*, No. 151, 1985, p. 84; reference [4] above.

[18] See L. Althusser, *For Marx*, London, Allen & Unwin, 1969. Also L. Althusser and E. Balibar, *Reading Capital*, translated by B. Brewster, London, New Left Books, 1970.

[19] L. Colletti, 'Marxism and the Dialectic', *New Left Review*, No. 93, 1975, pp. 3–29. Translated by J. Mathews, p. 29.

[20] Ibid., p. 29.

[21] Ibid., p. 29.

[22] I. Meszaros, *Marx's Theory of Alienation*, London, Merlin Press, 1971, p. 96.

[23] D. McLellan, *Marx's Grundrisse*, London, Macmillan, 1971, p. 13.

[24] K. Marx, *Theses on Feuerbach*, 1845. The Theses can be found in T. Bottomore & M. Rubel, *Karl Marx on Sociology and Social Philosophy*, Harmondsworth, Penguin, 1971.

[25] L. Colletti, op. cit., p. 29.

[26] Colletti does not accept that it is a viable option to try to establish

'dialectical materialism' as a distinct kind of theory. He bases his argument upon the distinction in formal logic between a logical contrary (which is an opposition of incompatible opposites which are not contradictory: 'A and B'), and a logical contradiction (an opposition which is based upon contradiction: 'A and not-A'). A dialectical contradiction is a logical contradiction and not real contrariety. Dialectical materialism has confused this, and seen contrariety in reality as contradictory, 'A and not-A', dialectical contradiction, instead of as contrary, 'A and B'. Colletti uses Kantian ideas, something criticized by Gramsci. See SPN, p. 389.

[27] SPN, p. 331; and p. 346.
[28] See M. Weber, *The Methodology of the Social Sciences*, translated by E. Shils *et al.*, Glencoe, Illinois, Free Press, chapter 1.
[29] Gramsci referred to most of Marx's works, including the *Civil War in France, Eighteenth Brumaire, The Poverty of Philosophy, Critique of the Gotha Programme, Preface to the 'Critique of Political Economy'*, and *Capital*. The *1844 Economic and Philosophic Manuscripts*, however, were not available until 1927 in Russian, the year Gramsci was imprisoned, and 1932 in German and French editions.
[30] K. Marx, *Critique of the Gotha Programme*, p. 21 of Foreign Language edition, Moscow, Foreign Languages Publishing House.
[31] Ibid., p. 22.
[32] L. Althusser, 1969, *op. cit.* in ref. [18] above.
[33] F. Engels, *Socialism: Utopian and Scientific*, English edition; 1959, Moscow, Foreign Languages Publishing House.
[34] Ibid., pp. 83–84.
[35] Ibid., p. 119.
[36] Ibid., p. 84.
[37] Ibid., p. 85.
[38] Ibid., p. 81.
[39] F. Engels, op. cit. in ref. [33], p. 76.
[40] Ibid., p. 120.
[41] Ibid., p. 121.
[42] Ibid., pp. 109–110.
[43] See E. Laclau & C. Mouffe, *Hegemony and Socialist Strategy. Towards a Radical Democratic Politics*, translated by W. Moore & P. Cammack, London, Verso Press, 1985.
[44] SPN, p. 238.
[45] SPN, p. 418.
[46] See Section III, 'The Philosophy of Praxis', in SPN, for example.
[47] SPN, p. 371.

[48] See G. Lukacs, 'Reification and the Consciousness of the Proletariat', in *History and Class Consciousness*, translated by R. Livingstone, Merlin Press, 1971, London. 'Any transformation can only come about as the product of the — free — action of the proletariat', p. 209.

4

Social change

The problematic of hegemony involves not only a new relationship between philosophy and sociology; it also includes a social theory about the part played by conceptions of the world and their associated values in social change. This emphasis constitutes a major similarity with that to be found in the work of Max Weber in spite of the political differences between the two writers. Weber did not share Gramsci's political commitment to socialism/communism but there are nevertheless some similarities in their social theories of change — a view which has been disputed by other commentators. The similarities and differences between the theories of Weber and Gramsci will be examined in this chapter, with specific reference to the analysis of the role of religions in historical change.

WEBER AND GRAMSCI

A central feature of Gramsci's work lies in the sophistication of his theoretical approach, especially when compared with the perspective of a crude version of historical materialism. He criticized historical materialism for being over-deterministic in predicting an inevitable change to a new mode of production, as if this change was built into history. For Gramsci, such an approach confuses nature and history; history is not a part of nature. The dogmatic version of historical materialism assumes that laws of history could be discovered which unfold automatically and independently of human intentions. Such teleological views of history lead to what Gramsci called 'fatalism', that is a resigned acceptance of whatever happens historically.[1]

Gramsci's approach to the critique of deterministic historical materialism is one which has some important similarities with that of Max Weber. Both of them stressed the importance of allowing some autonomy to the political and cultural levels. Weber and Gramsci both saw the economic as a fundamental background level in the analysis of large-scale historical change, but they conceptualized it in different ways. In the case of Weber, the economic was conceptualized as being a form of action which gave rise to classes based upon the ownership of the main forms of property in an economy — such as land, animals, water, money, mines, machines, factories, distribution networks — and upon the market situation of other classes in the occupational sphere. The market situation of a group in modern capitalism varied from that of the highly qualified with a marketable skill, who could command a high salary and a high degree of security; to 'formally free' wage labour, with varying degrees of capacity to extract high wages, and protection from unemployment; to the unskilled, casually employed, labourers who were paid low wages and could easily be made redundant. The specific type of modern capitalism of interest to Weber was defined by him as that form of the rational and peaceful pursuit of profit which typified all forms of capitalism as distinct from adventurism, and which was based upon a unique feature — 'the rational capitalistic organization of (formally) free labour'.[2] That is to say that the growth of the modern proletariat became the distinguishing feature of modern forms of capitalism; such a labour force differentiates modern capitalism from slave-owning systems, from serfdom, and from peasant-based economies.

Weber was explicit that he thought that the economic factor was of fundamental importance in the explanation of Western rationalism:

> It is . . . our first concern to work out and to explain genetically the special peculiarity of Occidental rationalism, and within this field that of the modern Occidental form. Every such attempt at explanation must, recognizing the fundamental importance of the economic factor, above all take account of the economic conditions'.[3]

Having made this clear, Weber then said that he wanted to explore the influence of cultural factors upon the motivation of the early modern bourgeoisie to engage in capitalist entrepreneurial activities:

> For though the development of economic rationalism is partly dependent on rational technique and law, it is at the same time determined by the ability and disposition of men to adopt certain types of practical rational conduct. When these types have been obstructed by spiritual obstacles, the development of rational economic conduct has also met serious inner resistance. The magical and religious forces, and the ethical ideas of duty based upon them, have in the past always been among the most important formative influences on conduct.[4]

Weber's work on the sociology of the world religions was geared to this overall objective of the assimilation of cultural factors, especially religious and moral conceptions of the world, in understanding and explaining the differences in the economic development of the Orient and the Occident. Weber was also interested in understanding and explaining the part cultural ideas and values played in the political sphere, and in the processes of legitmation of the ruling groups in a state. The political sphere was based upon a material factor for Weber, as for Gramsci, namely the control over the means of violence in a given territory. Weber wrote:

> Ultimately, one can define the modern state sociologically in terms of the specific means peculiar to it, as to every political association, namely, the use of physical force. . . . 'Every state is founded on force', said Trotsky at Brest-Litovsk. That is indeed right.[5]

The state is a relation in which one group dominates another group, Weber argued:'If the state is to exist, the dominated must obey the authority claimed by the powers that be . . . Upon what inner justifications and upon what external means does this domination rest?'[6]

Weber introduced his three well-known analytical types of legitimation to answer this question. It may be recalled that these were: traditional forms of legitimation, based upon ancient mores and an 'habitual orientation to conform'; charismatic, based upon the extraordinary and personal gift of grace and other qualities imputed to the leader; and finally, rational-legal, based upon rationally created rules, which must be obeyed if legal sanctions are to be avoided.[7]

Gramsci's work on hegemony was equally concerned with cultural, religious, philosophical and moral factors, set within a wider theoretical model which included the economic mode of production as fundamental but not fully determining. Gramsci also included the political element, especially the state's coercive force, in his model for the analysis of modern capitalism. Gramsci argued that there was a distinction between 'domination' in a state based upon force, and 'leadership' based upon hegemonic consent. Gramsci wrote:

> the supremacy of a social group manifests itself in two ways, as 'domination' and as 'intellectual and moral leadership'. A social group dominates antagonistic groups, which it tends to 'liquidate', or to subjugate by armed force: it leads kindred and allied groups.[8]

A similar conceptual distinction between 'domination' based upon force, and 'consent', a willingness to obey based upon moral and intellectual leadership (Gramsci), or inner justification and external means (Weber), operates in the two theories. The major concepts of Gramsci and Weber are congruent, even if they derive from two different political perspectives on the relative stability of modern capitalism, and upon the merits of socialism. Weber, unlike Gramsci, saw socialism as the extension of rational action into economic affairs, rather than as constituting a major break with capitalism and, thereby, providing the foundations for a new type of civilization which would become possible under full communism.

The view that there are theoretical and conceptual similarities between Gramsci and Weber is rejected by those commentators upon Gramsci who wish to stress his political differences with Weber, arguing that as a Marxist Gramsci must be seen as having worked within a different problematic from that of Weber.[9] This rigorous distinction which some maintain between Gramscian Marxism and Weberian sociology is based upon the political differences between the two theorists. The importance of making rigorous distinctions between different 'problematics' which are related to differing political outlooks can be carried too far, however. Certainly the major thrust of Gramsci's position was to try to find the positive elements in the work of writers who might differ from him politically and to aim to build upon these.[10]

Other writers, such as Habermas for example, have argued that it is important to maintain a logical distinction between intellectual, scientific discussion and those debates which are porimarily about political strategy and aims.[11] This position is coherent and useful, and one which is compatible with Gramsci's, in that Habermas argued that social theory ought to be treated as being autonomous from day-to-day political strategy.

It should be emphasized that both Weber and Gramsci recommended a similar approach intellectually to the analysis of long-term historical change, an approach which stressed the importance of conceptions of the world in understanding historical changes. For both of them, views-of-the-world, religions, moral values and motivational patterns were important in understanding historical change, even though neither of them denied the role of economic material interests, nor of physical force. They both opposed dogmatic historical materialism in their writings — indeed this could be said to have been the main thrust in both writers.

Nevertheless Gramsci was working on the basis of his rational commitment to the philosophy of praxis, a dialectical conception of Marxism, which was far removed from Weber's neo-positivism. Weber tried to maintain a distinction between value-judgements and value-relevance, a distinction which became difficult, if not impossible, to sustain over time.

The issue which Weber never addressed satisfactorily was that of the truth value of specific world-views, philosophies, or moral value systems. He thought that there was no rational way of choosing between world-views and was to this extent a relativist, or even an existentialist, in that he saw that a commitment to a world-view was necessary, especially for those who were active politically, but held that no universally valid rational grounds could be given for any particular commitment.[12]

There is in Gramsci a careful avoidance of the cruder types of both neo-positivism and historical materialism, neither of which conceptualize political action satisfactorily in his view. In the cruder forms of historical materialism criticized by Gramsci, political action is conceptualized as being action which reflects the imputed material interests of a class, or class fraction, located in terms of its position in the economic structure. Gramsci points out that there is a difficulty:

> in identifying at any given time, statically (like an instantaneous photographic image) the structure. Politics in fact is at any given time the reflection of the tendencies of development in the structure, but it is not necessarily the case that these tendencies must be realised. A structural phase can be concretely studied and analysed only after it has gone through its whole process of development, and not during the process itself, except hypothetically . . . From this it can be deduced that a particular political act may have been an error of calculation on the part of the leaders of the dominant classes . . . Mechanical historical materialism does not allow for the possibility of error, but assumes that every political act is determined, immediately, by the structure, and therefore as a real and permanent (in the sense of achieved) modification of the structure . . . .[13]

Weber had opposed mechanical historical materialism too. His alternative substantive model of modern societies was not satisfactory, however, when compared to that of the more coherent model of Marxists, it has been argued by F. Parkin, a critic otherwise sympathetic to Weber.

> Having in effect abandoned the distinction between capital and labour as the defining elements of class, Weber never proposes an alternative model. That is, he sets out no principles by which to locate the notional 'boundary' between a dominant or exploiting class and a subordinate or exploited class. What is portrayed

instead is a Hobbesian war of all against all as each group fights for
its own corner in the anarchy of the market place.[14]

There is, however, a definition of property classes in Weber:
' "Property" and "lack of property" are, therefore, the basic categories of
all class situations'.[15] As was seen above, there is a definition of the
working class in Weber, in terms of formally free labour. This may not be
the precise definition of class in Marxism, but a definition which holds in all
the places where Marx writes about classes is difficult, if not impossible, to
find within Marx too. The definition Weber gave is a rough rule of thumb, a
working definition.

Weber mentioned other bases of stratification such as status groups —
ethnicity and caste being major examples of this form of stratification built
upon differential amounts of 'status honour' or esteem. Weber also
examined the role of political parties and state bureaucracies in the
distribution of power and authority in a society, in addition to the power
conferred on those who owned substantial property in the economy.[16]
These additional bases of stratification are ones with which Gramsci was
also concerned.[17] Gramsci had a similar awareness of the role of political
parties, and the state, to that of Weber. Both were concerned with
establishing the autonomy of the political as a dimension which could not be
simply deduced from economic material interests of groups, or classes.
They both stressed that 'ideal' interests existed too; that is that classes and
status groups were carriers of conceptions of the world, of solutions to the
problem of meaning in Weberian terms, which could influence their actions
and their view of their own material interests. Gramsci expressed his view
of how stratification, including gender differences, affect religious beliefs,
values and practices in the following way for example:

> Every religion, even Catholicism . . . is in reality a multiplicity of
> distinct and often contradictory religions: there is one Catholicism
> for the peasants, one for women, and one for intellectuals which is
> itself variegated and disconnected.[18]

Gramsci might well be called the 'Weber of Marxism' in that he drew
attention to the social, political and cultural factors which need to be
introduced into the economistic Marxist model for the analysis of social and
economic change. On substantive political issues the two theorists did differ
as a consequence of their different philosophical positions — Gramsci
being optimistic that a human, democratic and modern form of socialism
was possible; Weber holding that socialism would not herald a new form of
civilization but the extension of rationality to all spheres of life, ending in

the bureaucratic state and a totally rationalized society, without any sense of mystery or awe, or of the sacred.

In spite of their political differences and their quite distinct hopes or fears about the future, the similarities between Weber and Gramsci cannot be overlooked or ignored. This is especially so if one is trying to build up a social theory about modern capitalism in a way which looks for links between theories in order to build up a wide intellectual alliance, rather than to reproduce the rigid boundaries of competing political sects within intellectual circles. Some of the similarities between Weber and Gramsci stem from a common intellectual, or philosophical, concern to distinguish the natural sciences, which conceptualize forces at work in the world of material objects and biological organisms, from the human sciences which are concerned with the purposes, goals and meanings involved in human action and with the unintended consequences of such action. Gramsci's criticism of deterministic interpretations of Marxism, such as that found in Bukharin, relies on a distinction between natural sciences and human sciences which reflects that found in Weber. The judgement of one recent writer, J. Femia, seems difficult to fault:

> Gramsci, in opposition to Bukharin, posits a cleavage between the domain of natural science and the world of human activity, so that the categories of the former cannot be applied to the latter. There is an irreducible difference between, on the one hand, the explanatory resources available to us in our dealings with natural phenomena and, on the other, those modes of understanding specifically adapted to the realm of human actions.

Femia also makes the point that human action cannot be fully understood or explained in purely quantitative terms because human action involves 'purposes, motives, acts of will, thoughts, hopes, fears, desires and so forth'.[19]

Not only is there a similarity between Gramsci and Weber with regard to their concerns with the autonomy of the political and of the importance, nevertheless, of the economic level in the understanding of a society and of historical change, and of the role of culture, including the various solutions of the problem of meaning to be found in the world religions; but also similar concrete issues concerned them both. Bureaucracy was one such concrete issue of concern to both theorists. A second substantive topic which both writers considered was the role of asceticism, especially in values concerned with sexuality and the construction of an ideology of work in modern capitalism. Each of these substantive issues will be discussed here briefly.

For Weber, the process of the increasing bureaucratization of more and more areas of life seemed inevitable, as rationalization continued to develop in modern capitalist, socialist and social democratic societies. Bureaucracies were set up to achieve values which had won widespread support among newly enfranchised groups, including the working classes and women, beginning in the late nineteenth and early twentieth centuries. Values such as justice and equality before the law, of universal, or near-universal, insurance schemes against sickness, unemployment and old age, state education for all — all these developments led to the modern welfare state. In industry and commerce, the processes of increasing rationalization led to bureaucratic methods overcoming familistic, traditional methods of staff recruitment, of financing and accounting and of planning future production, distribution and marketing. An increasing amount of bureaucratization was to be found in both capitalism and in socialism, on Weber's analysis.

There was no disjunction for Weber between modern, rational capitalism and socialism. Rather socialism appeared as a further extension of bureaucratic rationality into more and more spheres of life, to achieve the values of equality, justice and welfare provision for all citizens.

Weber's assessment of the inevitability of increasing bureaucratization in all types of modern societies left him ambivalent about the consequences of such a process for human beings. On the one hand nobody of liberal disposition, such as Weber, could fail to welcome the extension of the values of justice, reasonable incomes, health, housing and welfare services to all in a society. This led to the setting up of more and more bureaucracies in the state and in private spheres in the case of capitalist societies. On the other hand he saw what he called an increasing 'de-magnification' of the world, a loss of the sacred dimension, and of the non-rational ('*entzauberung der Welt*').[20] This process Weber thought was inevitable, at least in the West, where the culture was driven by rationality in all major spheres. It would lead, however, to the loss of a sense of the non-rational in existence, of spontaneity, novelty, and unpredictability, which Weber regretted.

The crucial element Weber did not see, and which remains the great divide between his generation and later ones of the twentieth century, was the rise of non-rational politics in Germany in the form of Nazism. It is this phenomenon which separates Weber from later modern sociologists and social theorists. The growth of Nazism led to a questioning of Weber's assessment of the inevitability of the increasing rationalization of modern existence and his view that the non-rational would disappear from modern industrial societies. Nazism can be seen as being in part a response to the de-magification of the modern world, with its rallies, symbolism, and celebration of war and violence, offering the re-magification of the world.

No sooner had Weber finished his work on the process of the increasing de-magification of the modern world, than World War One broke out. Not magic, but violence on an unprecedented scale, interrupted the process of the increasing rationalization of the modern world, which Weber had characterized as being peaceful development within modern, sober, rational capitalism. Following that war in Italy first, then in Germany, the non-rational irrupted into national and international politics, at the level of fascist ideology, in the practices of anti-semitism and in another world war.

Although Gramsci did not address Nazism as such in his writings he experienced Italian fascism directly. This experience gives his theory a depth which cannot be expected from the generation which died before the nineteen-thirties and forties.[21] Gramsci remained optimistic, even in an Italian fascist jail, in striking contrast to Weber's pessimism about the future as being one of an increasingly bureaucratized existence in modern states. Gramsci addressed the problem of 'bureaucratic centralism' in the *Prison Notebooks* and sought a solution in philosophy and praxis to this phenomenon which he saw developing in the Soviet Union under Stalin.[22] 'Democratic centralism' was Gramsci's offered solution, in which there would be an elite of leaders who could educate the mass membership of the party. Crucially, for Gramsci, the leadership must develop methods of listening to, and really responding to, the masses. This must occur before the revolution if bureaucratic centralism was to be avoided after it. His notion of the party was that it constituted a new state in embryo, not merely one more electoral party hoping to win an election. The methods of leadership which the party developed under capitalism were central in affecting, or determining, the state structures under socialism. Democratic centralism was intended to avoid dictatorship by a group, or one leader, before and after the revolution. Gramsci, interestingly, never used the term 'the dictatorship of the proletariat' in the *Prison Notebooks*.[23]

Gramsci's view of bureaucracy was that it was an essential feature in modern societies, a view Weber held too, but Gramsci thought that it could be brought under democratic control. Here his experience with the factory councils in Turin in the early nineteen-twenties had some bearing on his later thinking, but he switched his attention to the party and away from the factory as the key organization in his strategy for change. Gramsci had written in 1919 that in 'the factory councils, the worker participates by virtue of his role as producer, i.e. in consequence of his universal character, in consequence of his function and position in society . . .'.[24] After the failure of the Turin and Milan factory councils in 1920, when the workers, having occupied the factories, then returned the factories to the employers, and started to work again, Gramsci moved on to consider the role of the party. The party was to be a source of education, following Lenin and Marx, neither of whom thought that the workers could 'spontaneously' develop socialism out of their experiences in factories. Gramsci did not see the educational role of the party as being one of political agitation and propaganda, as Lenin had done, but as Femia has put it, he 'conceived the solution in broad ethical and cultural terms'.[25] The party was to impart ethical and cultural values, not merely watered-down theory and tactics, to the workers. Gramsci remained optimistic that such education of the workers was possible, and that over-bureaucratization of the party, in the sense of a central group handing down instructions to be followed by those lower down the system, could be avoided without any great loss in effectiveness.

There are parallels between Gramsci and Weber with regard to their respective analyses of the increasing rationalization of work and the disciplines necessary for work in modern industry. Gramsci was interested especially in what he termed 'Fordism', that is the methods and associated disciplines, introduced into the factories of the Ford Motor Company in the United States in the early decades of the twentieth century. Gramsci linked his comments about work discipline with remarks about the law prohibiting alcohol in the United States, which was passed in 1922. He wrote:

> In America rationalization of work and prohibition are undoubtedly connected. The enquiries conducted by the industrialists into the workers' private lives and the inspection services created by some firms to control the 'morality' of their workers are necessities of the new methods of work. People who laugh at these initiatives (failures though they were) and see in them only a hypocritical manifestation of 'puritanism' thereby deny themselves any possibility of understanding the importance, significance and objective import of the American phenomenon, which is also the biggest collective effort to date to create, with unprecedented speed, and with a consciousness of purpose unmatched in history, a new type of worker and man.[26]

> [Gramsci continued:] The sexual question is again connected with that of alcohol. Abuse and irregularity of sexual functions is, after alcoholism, the most dangerous enemy of nervous energies . . . .

> Someone who works for a wage, with fixed hours, does not have time to dedicate himself to the pursuit of drink or to sport or to evading the law. The same observation can be made about

sexuality. 'Womanising' demands too much leisure . . . The exaltation of passion cannot be reconciled with the timed movements of productive motions connected with the most perfected automation.[27]

These remarks echo those of Weber, in his essay, *The Protestant Ethic and the Spirit of Capitalism*, and his work on the *Sociology of Religion*. For example, Weber argued that:

Rational ascetic alertness, self-control, and methodical planning of life are seriously threatened by the peculiar irrationality of the sexual act, which is ultimately and uniquely unsusceptible to rational organization.[28]

Weber was also concerned with the stamp left on specific religious messages as a result of the carriers, or bearers, of diverse religious movements, having had different experiences of work and a variety of relationships with nature. This included the religious needs, for example, of peasants, state rulers, capitalists, military classes and castes, manual workers, and intellectual strata in state and religious organizations. This theme is echoed in Gramsci as will be seen in considering his work on religion more generally in the next section of this chapter.

RELIGION IN GRAMSCI AND WEBER

The blurring of the distinction between three fundamental concepts, namely those of the economic, the state and civil society, which is present in Gramsci's own writings and in some later developments, notably in the work of Althusser, has hindered the generation of an adequate recognition in Gramscian social theory of the part which religions play in many contemporary societies. The influence of religion can be seen, for instance, in the most industrially developed capitalist society, the United States, where both right-wing evangelical Christians and some Roman Catholics have been active in national and local politics. They have formed pressure groups which seek to reassert moral and legal controls over a series of issues from prayers and the teaching of the theory of biological evolution in schools, to wider issues such as abortion and homosexuality. Britain has seen similar politically active religious pressure groups which have arisen in the last two decades, as in the attempt to control pornography, the pressure to increase the policing of male homosexuals, the opposition to contraception being available to young people and opposition to abortion.[29]

It was pointed out in Chapter 1 that there were three distinct models about the relations between the economy, the state and civil society, which can be found in Gramsci's *Prison Notebooks*. These have been distinguished and discussed by P. Anderson.[30] Althusser used one of these models, the one which collapsed together the concepts of 'civil society' and the 'state', retaining the 'economy' as the other fundamental concept.[31] This althusserian conflation of the notions of state and civil society was made in the conceptualization of 'ideological state apparatuses' and 'repressive state apparatuses'.[32] In much of Gramsci's work, on the other hand, the state as a coercive instrument is seen as being distinct from those institutions of civil society which are concerned with morals and philosophy. Some states, Gramsci recognized, have taken on the tasks of raising the level of civilization among the people, but this was less typical of modern capitalist societies. There is an ambiguity here, a shift in the definition of the state as based upon solely coercive power, and the state as involved in educational processes for instance. This ambiguity about the distinction between the state and civil society has led to problems in understanding the concept of hegemony and of the political strategy to be derived from it.

In what I think is the most theoretically coherent analytical model of hegemony which Gramsci developed, hegemony is conceived of as being exercised in the economy, in factories and offices, in the state, especially in law and the legal process and in state educational institutions, and in civil society, in the mass media and the arts, and in religions. This analytical model of hegemony contains the concept of a class, or an alliance of classes and class fractions, able to lead intellectually and politically in all three spheres. In any given historical situation hegemony is only going to be found as the partial exercise of leadership of the dominant class, or alliance of class fractions, in some of these spheres but not in all of them equally successfully all the time. To suppose otherwise is to fail to distinguish the analytical model of hegemony from the analysis of concrete cases. In other words, the degree of hegemonic leadership which is successfully provided by a ruling group, or alliance, can vary from a relatively fully integrated situation, at one end of the continuum, in which all classes and groups give their consent to the leading hegemonic arrangements in the economy and in philosophy and morals, through to a situation in which there is an almost total lack of leadership being provided by the ruling group outside of the upper classes. There is an intermediate position in which some degree of integration of all the classes and groups takes place, including the working classes in modern capitalism, but where this integration is by no means complete. Resistance and dissent find some expression, Gramsci argued, but in a confused way, without intellectual order, as in many strikes in Italy in his own lifetime for example.[33]

It is not helpful to fuse the concept of civil society with that of the state in the manner of Althusser's 'ideological state apparatuses', for this blurs a theoretically and politically useful distinction between those social and cultural institutions over which a state may exercise direct financial control, and may determine these organizations' activities quite directly, from those social and cultural institutions which are almost entirely autonomous of the state. An important example of the latter type of institution in civil society is religion, especially in those cases in which the religious leaders are not linked with the state in any direct way as they are in an 'established church' such as the Church of England, or even more so as they were in the case of the Russian Orthodox Church in pre-revolutionary Russia.

Religious organizations and movements do have a considerable degree of autonomy from the state in many modern capitalist social formations.[34] The important point here is that it is useful to preserve the conception of the possibility of some social institutions being relatively autonomous of the state and therefore capable of operating in civil society — a zone which is conceptualized as being a distinct and separate one from that of the state. Furthermore both the state and civil society are conceptualized as being potentially, if not always in actual concrete cases, autonomous of the economic sphere.

For Gramsci, religions are seen to operate as popularly based world-views, with a moral value system, a related belief system and a symbolic/ritual system. Western Christianity, in particular, has an organisational base in churches, denominations and sects, together with a clear educational programme often pursued in its own schools in the past. It has had some success historically in operating hegemonically, providing both the leading moral value system, which has been enshrined frequently in state laws, and in the main world-view among the masses in parts of Europe and in North and Latin America for instance. Religion, on Gramsci's view, provides a relatively incoherent, but nevertheless an operative, world-view to millions of people who are socialized into it.

Gramsci argued that:

> Religion and common sense cannot constitute an intellectual order, because they cannot be reduced to unity and coherence even within an individual consciousness, let alone collective consciousness. Or rather they cannot be so reduced 'freely' — for this may be done by 'authoritarian' means, indeed within limits this has been done in the past.[35]

Religious specialists, such as bishops, priests, preachers and evangelists, may provide support to ruling groups in particular states, or they may be critical of them and of some of their actions. Religion may be called 'ideology', if the word 'ideology' is used in:

> its highest sense of a conception of the world that is implicitly manifest in art, in law, in economic activity and in all manifestations of individual and collective life. [Any conception of the world has to preserve] the ideological unity of the entire social bloc which that ideology serves to cement and to unify.[36]

Gramsci refers to the Roman Catholic Church as one example of a religious organization which still, in the nineteen-thirties, managed more successfully than Marxism to integrate intellectuals and the ordinary masses into one relatively unified world-view, moral system and organization. A philosophical movement must seek to link the intellectuals and the masses organically together if it is to be more than a movement of ideas among intellectuals and consequently ineffective in influencing politics.

The concept of 'politics' is understood very broadly by Gramsci here. It includes all aspects of social life, from the family, the arts, economic activities, education and writing, to the state and law. 'Politics', on this definition, is an area that coincides with that covered by the whole of Catholicism's moral theology. Intellectual ideas should not remain at a purely cognitive level, written in texts, but become socially and politically formative among the masses by providing the basis of a lived morality.

It is politics which provides the link between the philosophy, or conception of the world, which is produced by intellectuals and by professional philosophers, often just one major individual philosopher, and ordinary people's 'common sense' conceptions of the world. There is an internal politics of those organizations that are concerned with religion and philosophy. Gramsci drew attention to the authoritarian manner in which religions, Catholicism in particular, have tried to control their intellectuals so that they do not become too removed from the masses' level of 'faith' which is simple and dogmatic. A party organization concerned with educating the masses into understanding the philosophy of praxis, on the other hand, should be able to encourage intellectuals to both explore ideas relatively freely and to be in contact with the masses and their problems, so that the intellectuals do not become removed from the problems of ordinary life but relate their philosophy to these problems.

> The philosophy of praxis does not tend to leave the 'simple' in their primitive philosophy of common sense, but rather to lead them to a higher conception of life. If it affirms the need for contact between intellectuals and simple it is not in order to

restrict scientific activity and preserve unity at the low level of the masses, but precisely to construct an intellectual-moral bloc which can make politically possible the intellectual progress of the mass and not only of small intellectual groups.[37]

Although Gramsci does not mention Weber at this point in his work on the relations between religious intellectuals, 'religious virtuosi' as Weber termed them, and the masses, or 'folk' in Weber's terms, there is a parallel between the two writers' analyses. Weber did not compare his analysis of the relations between the virtuosi and the folk in religions with that of political leaders and the masses directly, as did Gramsci. However, some similarities are present. In *The Sociology of Religion*[38] Weber was concerned with the influence intellectuals had exerted on the development of world religions and their role in politics. Weber wrote:

The destiny of religions has been influenced in a most comprehensive way by intellectualism and its various relationships to the priesthood and political authorities. These relationships were in turn influenced by the provenience of the class which happened to be the carrier of the particular intellectualism.[39]

As was mentioned above, Weber also analysed the influence of the poor, the lower middle classes, peasants, the bourgeoisie, aristocracies, the military, and state rulers, upon world religions, but the specific focus he gave to the role of intellectuals, and their social relationships with non-intellectual strata, does have a similarity with Gramsci's interests in the relations between religious and political intellectuals and the masses. Indeed, Gramsci does refer to Weber's study of Calvinism and the development of rational capitalism explicitly as an example of the influence of religion providing 'a specific way of rationalising the world and real life, which provided the general framework for real practical activity'.[40] This was in the context of an argument Gramsci was developing against mechanistic determinism, 'fatalism', within Marxism, found in particular in the work of Burkharin on sociology, which he saw as a typical conception of 'subaltern' strata, the 'popular masses', but not of intellectuals. He uses the sociology of religion in order to provide a parallel set of examples of intellectual and mass types of faith to those which had developed within Marxism. Gramsci's main aim was to point out that fatalistic beliefs develop when a movement is being unsuccessful.[41]

Gramsci was concerned with arguing that Marxism needed an elite who were to be well educated in philosophy and political economy, but who would also be in touch with the masses and not only with other intellectuals.

Such 'organic intellectuals' would be able to relate to the working classes, the peasants, and to those in the middle classes who were disaffected by the dominant form of political ideology, which for much of Gramsci's lifetime was fascism. This view was one which Gramsci developed in opposition to that of mechanistic determinism, to the passive fatalism of waiting for the revolution to arrive, which was found among communists in the nineteen-twenties and -thirties.

Hegemony, in the sense of intellectual, philosophical leadership, had to be actively produced in Gramsci's view, and did not depend upon having taken power in the state. Hegemony could be built up, in some circumstances, in civil society even if not in either the state or the economy. Hence it is important to retain the notion of hegemony as being based in civil society if Gramsci's political position is to be properly understood.

Italian catholicism played a large part in Gramsci's analysis of the role of an orgnization of intellectuals and masses in producing hegemony for a particular conception of the world. Catholicism was seen, by Gramsci, as a model to be in part emulated, but whose mistakes were to be avoided. One of these mistakes has been mentioned above, namely the authoritarian controls the Catholic Church exercised over its intellectuals. This had taken the form of producing an Index which listed those books judged unfit for Catholics to read. The Church had also tried to prevent the publication of texts written by some of its members which were disapproved of by the Vatican. It is worth noting here that this practice was still being continued by the Vatican in the nineteen-eighties.

A basic error in the teachings and practices of Catholicism, Gramsci argued, was the belief that evil was located in the individual, not in social structures.

> From the 'philosophical' point of view, what is unsatisfactory in Catholicism is the fact that, in spite of everything, it insists on putting the cause of evil in the individual man himself, or in other words that it conceives of man as a defined and limited individual.[42]

It is important to note here a point omitted by Gramsci, namely that the Catholic Church has developed a set of social teachings set out in Papal encyclicals, from *Rerum Novarum* (1891) to *Quadragesimo Anno* (1931), and after Gramsci's own lifetime in *Populorum Progressio* (1967) for instance. These encyclicals have been critical of liberal capitalism as producing 'the international imperialism of money'.[43] However, these encyclicals did not develop a sustained position which might be termed 'Christian socialism', rather they were critical of it.

In the encyclical *Quadragesimo Anno* (*The Social OPrder*, 1931) Pope Pius XI stated:

> We do not think it is necessary to warn upright and faithful children of the Church against the impious and nefarious character of communism.[44]

> Religious socialism, Christian socialism, are expressions implying a contradiction in terms. No one can be at the same time a sincere Catholic and a socialist properly so called.[45]

This attack by the Roman Catholic Church upon socialism has been softened in the years since the ending of fascism in Italy. This may be as a consequence of the growth of a larger urban working class in Italy, France, Spain, Portugal and the countries in Latin America, among whom the Catholic Church has lost influence. In recent years socialism has been less openly attacked, capitalism more so, as in the 1967 encyclical of Pope Paul VI:

> But if it is true that a type of capitalism has been the source of excessive suffering, injustices and fratricidal conflicts whose effects still persist, it would also be wrong to attribute to industrialization itself evils that belong to the woeful system which accompanied it.[46]

Nevertheless, it is the case that morality still largely impinges upon the ordinary church member as an individualistic set of rules of conduct, as Gramsci argued. 'Sin' is seen as being predominantly an individual act requiring absolution among most members of the churches, rather than, or even as well as, the maintenance of a set of social, economic and political structures which produce inhuman lives.[47]

By taking the example of Italian Catholicism as a basis for his anlysis of a relatively successful religious form of hegemony in civil society, Gramsci was able to point to the type of intellectual and moral leadership he had in mind for Marxism in civil society, before having the state's coercive power, or the state's capacity to effect hegemonic consent through its influence upon education and law for example, in the hands of the Communist Party. Gramsci saw Catholicism as something to be both taken seriously as a moral and religious conception of the world which still held great sway over many Italian peasants, and as an adversary in the struggle for the hearts and minds of the Italian people. This was during the period of fascism in Italy, when the Catholic Church was condemnatory towards socialism and communism, the two sources of potentially effective opposition to fascism.

It has been suggested in this chapter that the Gramscian concept of hegemony led to an analysis of the role of religion, especially in Italian society, as being autonomous of capitalist economic class interests in particular. This marked a degree of intellectual progress from cruder forms of Marxist analysis of religion as being ideological in the sense of serving narrow economic class interests. Gramsci's analysis had some striking parallels to the sociology of religion developed by Weber, especially in the attention it gave to beliefs, values, rituals and symbols as being, in some circumstances at least, autonomous in relation to economic class interests and to the relationship between religion and political rulers.

Gramsci's problematic of hegemony has been developed by two recent writers, Ernesto Laclau and Chantal Mouffe, in a direction which leads to what these writers call 'post-Marxism'. This development continues to echo, implicitly but not explicitly, certain of Weber's themes. These include issues such as the autonomy of moral values, especially values about economic and political conduct, together with an emphasis on political practices as being independent of economic class interests, narrowly conceived.[48] Laclau and Mouffe's viewpoint will be discussed in the next chapter. It is a position which has moved a long way from orthodox Marxist–Leninist positions, towards pluralism and democratic radicalism at the political level.

REFERENCES

[1] See 'Critical Notes on an attempt at Popular Sociology', in A. Gramsci, *Selections from the Prison Notebooks,* edited and translated by Q. Hoare & G. Nowell Smith, London, Lawrence & Wishart, 1971, pp. 419–472 (=SPN).

[2] M. Weber, *The Protestant Ethic and the Spirit of Capitalism,* London, Allen & Unwin, 1971, p. 21.

[3] Ibid., p. 26.

[4] Ibid., p. 26–27.

[5] M. Weber, 'Politics as a Vocation', in H. Gerth & C. Wright Mills (eds) *From Max Weber*, London, Routledge & Kegan Paul, 1970, pp. 77–78. I must point out how this quotation illustrates that Weber followed the methodological approach which Gramsci recommended, namely that of trying to find the positive aspects in other people's approaches!

[6] Ibid., p. 78.

[7] Ibid., p. 79.

[8] SPN, p. 58.

[9] See C. Buci-Glucksmann, *Gramsci and the State,* London, Lawrence & Wishart, 1980, p. 57 and note 32, p. 409. Earlier R. Milliband, *The State in Capitalist Society,* London, 1969, had argued that there were major similarities between Gramsci's concept of hegemony and Weber's conception of legitimation. This is rejected by Buci-Glucksmann, op. cit.

[10] See SPN, pp. 343–344. 'In the formulation of historico-critical problems it is wrong to conceive of scientific discussion as a process at law in which there is an accused and a public prosecutor whose professional duty it is to demonstrate that the accused is guilty and has to be put out of circulation. In scientific discussion, since it is assumed that the purpose of discussion is the pursuit of truth and the progress of science, the person who shows himself most 'advanced' is the one who takes up the point of view that his adversary may well be expressing a need which should be incorporated, if only as a subordinate aspect, in his own construction'.

[11] See J. Habermas, *Towards a Rational Society,* London, Heinemann, 1971.

[12] See J. Habermas, *Legitimation Crisis,* London, Heinemann, 1976, p. 97.

[13] SPN, p. 408.

[14] See F. Parkin, *Max Weber,* London, Tavistock, and Chichester, Ellis Horwood, 1982, p. 94.

[15] M. Weber, *Economy and Society,* New York, Bedminster Press, 1968, p. 927. Discussed by F. Parkin, op. cit., p. 92.

[16] See M. Weber, 'Politics as a Vocation', op. cit. in ref. [5] above.

[17] This is not mentioned by F. Parkin, op. cit. in ref. [14] above, in his discussion.

[18] SPN, p. 420.

[19] See J. Femia, *Gramsci's Political Thought,* Oxford, Clarendon Press, 1981, p. 75.

[20] See M. Weber, 1971, op. cit. in ref. [2] above.

[21] There is one reference to Hitler's *Mein Kampf* made by Gramsci, see SPN, p. 266.

[22] See J. Femia, op. cit., pp. 158–159.

[23] Ibid., p. 165.

[24] Gramsci article in 'L'Ordine Nuovo', 1919. See J. Femia, op. cit., pp. 141–142.

[25] J. Femia, op. cit., p. 156.

[26] SPN, p. 302.

[27] SPN, pp. 304–305.

[28] M. Weber, *The Sociology of Religion,* translated by E. Fischoff, London, Mthuen, 1966, chapter XIV, 'The Relationship of Religion to Politics, Economics, Sexuality, and Art', p. 238.

[29] See J. Weeks, *Sex, Politics and Society,* London, Longman, 1981, chapter 14.

[30] See P. Anderson, 'The Antimonies of Antonio Gramsci', in *New Left Review,* no. 100, 1976/77, pp. 5–78.

[31] See also C. Buci-Glucksmann, 1980, op. cit. in ref. [9].

[32] L. Althusser, *Lenin and Philosophy,* London, New Left Books, 1971.

[33] See J. Femia, op. cit. in ref. [19], pp. 46–48.

[34] The cases of the Church of England, and the Church of Scotland within modern Britain, both of which are established churches and whose head is the monarch, are rather exceptional among modern capitalist social formations.

[35] SPN, p. 326.

[36] SPN, p. 328.

[37] SPN, pp. 332–333.

[38] M. Weber, *The Sociology of Religion,* chapter VIII, 'Intellectualism, Intellectuals, and the History of Religion' — (1922), translated by E. Fischoff, London, Methuen, 1965.

[39] Ibid., p. 118.

[40] SPN, pp. 337–338 on Calvinism: 'The position of Calvinism, however, with its iron conception of predestination and grace, which produces a vast expansion of the spirit of initiative (or becomes the form of this movement) is even more revealing and significant'.

[41] See SPN, p. 337.

[42] SPN, p. 352.

[43] Pope Paul VI, *Populorum Progressio,* (English title: *The Great Social Problem*) London, Catholic Truth Society, 1967, p. 15 of English edition.

[44] Pope Pious XI, *Quadragesimo Anno,* p. 44 of English edition, London, Catholic Truth Society, 1960, paragraph 112.

[45] Ibid., p. 48, paragraph 120.

[46] Pope Paul VI, *Populorum Progressio* (*The Great Social Problem*) London, Catholic Truth Society, 1967, p. 15.

[47] See Pope Paul VI, *Humanae Vitae* (*On Human Life*), London, Catholic Truth Society, 1968.

[48] E. Laclau and C. Mouffe, *Hegemony and Socialist Strategy,* translated by W. Moore and P. Cammack, London, Verso Press, 1985. There is one reference to Weber's '*entzauberung der Welt*' in Laclau and Mouffe, see p. 94. Weber's name did not appear in the Index to the 1985 edition, however.

5

Hegemony and recent social theory

The problematic of hegemony has become important in political thought and practice of the last two decades outside Italy, especially in France, Spain and Britain. An example of this may be found in the recent work of the co-authors, Ernesto Laclau and Chantal Mouffe. This work, which has been influenced by the problematic of Gramsci, is discussed in the first section of this chapter, with special attention being given to their critique of essentialism. In particular, Laclau and Mouffe are concerned to provide a critique of the 'essentialist' forms of thinking, and of its associated political practices, to be found, in their view, on the left in both Eastern and Western Europe. Their critique concerns essentialist conceptions of the working class and, more generally, of the economic base, which are held by many on the left. Classes, they argue, are not to be found as already in existence but have to be produced through political activities. Members of economic classes do not simply know their material interests but have to form conceptions of them. This they do by using ideas and values found in the language and world-outlook of their period and culture, at least according to Gramsci. Nor are economic classes the only potential agents of change in modern conditions for Laclau and Mouffe. Other groups are organized now to seek to achieve change in the social, economic and legal situation of women, homosexuals, blacks and other ethnic minorities, for instance.

In the second major section of this chapter the question is raised of whether or not such an anti-essentialist philosophical position as that underlying Laclau and Mouffe's position is necessarily the one implicitly, or explicitly, to be found in Marx and, more importantly, whether or not it is an adequate basis for constructing an hegemonic moral and political philosophy in modern Western societies. The main argument will be that Marx did have a view of human nature which cannot be as easily ignored or dismissed as some anti-essentialists suggest without distorting Marx's philosophical and political position. Any conception of human nature has been highly criticized and eschewed by those adopting an anti-essentialist position. Some writers have argued, however, that an adequate political and moral philosophy must, logically, provide some account of the view of human nature upon which it is based. Unless a view of human nature is provided in a philosophy, or world-outlook, it risks collapsing into relativism. Such a world-view could not become hegemonic by a process of building consent in a non-coercive manner for it would not possess any coherent arguments to persuade people why certain changes are necessary if human beings are to become more cooperative, less aggressive, and more satisfied with their lives across the globe.

LACLAU AND MOUFFE ON HEGEMONY

Hegemony has become a fundamental concept for a new, radical democratic politics in the work of E. Laclau and C. Mouffe.[1] Basically they see Gramsci as having broken with the notion of the working class as the only, or central, social agency for revolution, a notion to be found in economistic versions of Marxism. They acknowledge, however, that Gramsci did retain a conception of the hegemony of the working class in alliance with other class fractions, forming an historic bloc. According to Laclau and Mouffe, the concept of 'historical bloc' enabled Gramsci to transcend the economistic view of the working class as arriving already constituted upon the historical stage, when the final crisis of capitalism arrived. Gramsci began to conceptualize politics as 'articulation', a process of the construction of political subjects by organically based intellectuals.[2] The need for a 'collective will' to be forged by 'intellectual and moral leadership', not only as in Lenin by the political leadership provided by the 'vanguard party', becomes 'the organic cement unifying a historical block' in the new conception of hegemony Gramsci developed.[3]

In order to situate the contribution of Laclau and Mouffe within the wider debate about the notion of hegemony it is necessary to look at how the conceptualization of class has developed in recent discussions. There has been a debate, conducted by some recent Marxists, about the definition and conceptualization of classes which is to be found in Marx's work.[4] The main problem in arriving at fixed definitions of 'class' is that such definitions depend upon the wider theoretical problematic of the social analyst. This theoretical problematic in turn is related to the political philosophy, and to the political goals and values of the social analyst. The 'working class', or proletariat, in Marxist theory, does not exist as a given, fixed entity. The concept of the proletariat may be used to refer only to the specific situation of wage-labourers in manufacturing, or extractive, indus tries, who are exploited, that is surplus-value is extracted from their labour by paying them less than the value they add to raw materials in a given time period.[5] Alternatively, anyone who has to sell their labour power in order to live, and owns little or no private property which could provide an income sufficient to sustain them, may be said to be members of the proletariat. This definition excludes the petit bourgeoisie, the industrial and financial capitalist classes, the land-owning class, and landlords of rented properties. It does, however, include occupational groups such as engineers, many public sector workers, teachers, and health service sector workers who would be excluded on the definition of the proletariat which is based upon the extraction of surplus-value in industrial production.

Whichever definition of the 'working class' is used, the decision to settle for one or the other partly depends upon the view taken of the theory of surplus-value. Some Marxists would now reject this concept as an inadequate economic theory while others still see it as being fundamental to the science of Marxism. The decision about the concept of surplus-value depends in turn upon how 'exploitation' is seen as being located — whether it is seen as being located only in the sphere of industrial production, or in other work situations more generally, or whether even consumption is seen as another potential area of exploitation. However, exploitation and surplus-value are seen and analysed, it is difficult indeed, near the end of the twentieth century, to argue that the workers in manufacturing industry in the advanced capitalist countries are the likely leaders of a revolution. In a crisis situation, some sections of the industrial working class may behave in a politically reactionary way, being attracted to non-rational, racialist ideologies for instance. It is because it is difficult to argue plausibly that the working classes of the United States, or of some western European societies, defined in the narrow way as the industrial workers involved in manufacturing and in the extraction of raw materials, will be the leaders of a revolutionary movement to overthrow capitalism, that some Marxists have turned to the wider definition of the working class mentioned above. At least this includes the majority of the wage-earning and salaried workers in modern societies, and although they may not be highly revolutionary either, this group, or class subject, is not so limited as it is in the narrow definition of the industrial proletariat.

Laclau and Mouffe go further and look to groups other than the economically 'exploited' classes in arguing that other forms of subordination exist outside the economic sphere. Subordination may be political, social or cultural, as well as economic, especially among groups such as women, ethnic minorities, gay people, and the old and sick.

Gramsci's importance lay in the fact that he emphasized that any 'class' has to be constructed in order to be historically and politically a potentially active agent. This process of the social construction of a class involves organic intellectuals actively helping to produce the class as a change agent. Classes do not arise already formed as agents of change within the relations of production. In concrete work situations workers will act usually in an economic-corporate way to protect their interests, but not to transform society, on Gramsci's view, which is itself congruent with those of both Marx and Lenin, as was discussed in the first chapter of this book.[6]

For Gramsci, other groups may be active in history-making processes too, especially political movements organized around an appeal to national self-determination for instance. A concrete instance of this, which Gramsci mentioned, was the movement for independence in India in the late nineteen-twenties and -thirties. Gramsci was thus one of the first major figures in Marxism to conceptualize the 'national-popular', to see the movements based on nationalism as change agents. Laclau and Mouffe extend this principle to include the social construction of other politically active agents, or subjects — including ethnic groups, women, homosexuals, protesters against nuclear weapons and environmentalists, for example.

Laclau and Mouffe go further, however, and maintain that it is necessary to break with any conception of society as having one hegemonic centre, an idea which Gramsci had retained from classical Marxism. Their position maintains that the concept of society as constituting a totality which is linked together, 'sutured', or stitched together, to form a unity of some kind, has to be abandoned. There is consequently no way of theorizing about determination in the last instance by the economic, in the way Althusser attempted to do for instance, because outside of an articulatory practice there are no social interconnections. They argue as follows:

> In order to place ourselves firmly within the field of articulation, we must begin by renouncing the conception of 'society' as founding totality of its partial processes. We must, therefore, consider the openness of the social as the constitutive ground or 'negative essence' of the existing, and the diverse 'social orders' as precarious and ultimately failed attempts to domesticate the field of differences . . . There is no sutured space peculiar to 'society', since the social itself has no essence.[7]

In other words any connections among groups in a society have to be constructed, articulated, and maintained; they do not arise automatically out of the mode of production, or out of any other component of a social formation. The mode of production does not exist in its own right, it is a conceptual, and social, construct, dependent upon legal private property rights for example and cannot be granted any ontological priority in reality.

Social, economic 'reality' is a construction made possible through articulatory practices. 'Articulatory practices' establish identities of elements through relation with other elements. '. . . All identity is relational . . .'.[8] There is no essence, no structure, which underlies the signifier. social identity is symbolic and relational, not fixed independently of any articulation.[9]

The realm of the symbolic becomes central for the position developed by Laclau and Mouffe, for it is here that subjects are constituted, as in the examples of nationalities, ethnic groups, women, and gay people. The term 'symbolic' is used here in place of 'ideology' in order to mark the intended break with the economic base–ideological superstructure model found persisting even in Althusser. However, this term, the 'symbolic', has to be understood not as having a purely linguistic reference, but as involving material practices, rituals, and institutions. 'Articulation' involves constructing 'nodal points' without which meaning and identity would slip away continually.

> The impossibility of an ultimate fixity of meaning implies that there have to be partial fixations — otherwise, the very flow of differences would be impossible. Even in order to differ, to subvert meaning, there has to be a meaning.[10]

Nodal points provide a partial fixation of meaning constructed by articulatory practices.

The Laclau/Mouffe position constitutes a major break with traditional Marxist conceptions, where the modes of production and of exchange are seen as the material base, existing in some sense independently of any conceptualizations of them. The capitalist mode of production and exchange is conceptualized as being a reality independent of people's intentions in classic forms of Marxism. Capitalism operates according to laws governing the extraction of surplus value, of profit, or of commodity production which remain independent of any groups' conceptions of them. A classic statement of this can be found in Engels's analysis in *Socialism: Utopian and Scientific* (1892), for instance:

> The new productive forces [of modern industry] have already outgrown the capitalistic mode of using them. And this conflict between productive forces and modes of production is not a conflict engendered in the mind of man, like that between original sin and divine justice. It exists, in fact, objectively, outside us, independently of the will and actions even of the men that have brought it on.[11]

Here it is important to point out that the break with traditional conceptions of Marxism, which is proposed in the work of Laclau and Mouffe, is virtually complete. The concepts of class, material base and ideological superstructure, of exploitation and surplus-value, the inevitability of crises in capitalism through over-production of commodities, of the withering away of the state, of proletarian revolution, all these conceptions and predictions are either explicitly rejected, or not even discussed, presumably because it is assumed that they are archaic and redundant concepts. One could argue that Laclau and Mouffe go further than Weber, for example, in moving away from material, economic factors. They stress the role of the symbolic alone in the processes of historical change.

There are two material practices, in particular, which were important in many forms of Marxism including that of Gramsci, and which are present also in Weber, but which are missing from Laclau and Mouffe's analysis. These are money, the cash nexus (originally a phrase of Carlyle's)[12] and the coercive practices of the state. These omissions relate to two major analytical components of the Gramscian problematic, namely, the state and its coercive power, and the economy, both the mode of production and of exchange. There are historically given social institutions and practices in the state, the economy, and in civil society, which have an important bearing upon political practices and possibilities for change in concrete social formations.

Coercive practices in the state, and the relations established by the cash nexus in the economy, both in production and exchange, could be seen as stitching the 'society' together to form a linked, or sutured, whole which is distinct from other societies stitched together elsewhere, *pace* Laclau and Mouffe. The practices which form the cash nexus — the flows of money which involve all members of modern capitalist countries — provide purely external links between people in a society. If this can be regarded as an 'articulatory practice' then there is no necessary problem for the Laclau and Mouffe analysis at this point. It is, however, difficult to conceptualize the cash nexus as such an articulatory practice. Rather it appears not as one additional articulation among others, but as an all-pervasive practice under modern conditions. Money operates impersonally and one might plausibly claim that it is an 'inarticulate practice'; that is to say that it obscures and mystifies relationships between people who communicate through money not through language, symbols and feelings. Money reduces all the relationships in which it is involved to a form of prostitution.

Furthermore, it is possible to define the boundaries of a society by tracing the area in which a particular currency may be used. Cash can be seen as a means of stitching, or suturing, a social formation together. Money, the cash nexus, played a central role in the analysis Marx gave of capitalism, for it allows the practices which produce the extraction of surplus value to take place. It cannot be lost quite as easily as is the case in the analysis made by Laclau and Mouffe without serious consequences, not the least of which is to build up false hopes about the ease with which change may occur within capitalism over the all-pervasive role of money, the cash-nexus, and ultimately capital itself. Capital is not going to disappear that easily.

The second material practice in a given territory which could be said to link, or stitch, disparate groups together, is the coercive power in the state as seen in policing activities, and behind these, the armed forces. The police and armed forces of a state operate as agents of social regulation. Law, and the processes of law enforcement, form a connecting thread, linking people to the state; law and policing are articulatory practices which go beyond verbal and ritualized discursive practices in police stations and courts; they move into the sphere of physical coercion as in most prisons, and in the assaults upon some citizens who are not involved in criminal activities as a full-time occupation. Groups such as peace protesters, often women, striking coal miners, and some blacks, to take some important examples from among groups not habituated to police violence in the past, all of these have complained about police harassment, and the use of unnecessary violence by some policemen in Britain in the early nineteen-eighties. The articulatory practices involved in law and punishment in a modern state do have a material component to them which cannot be overlooked as easily as the Laclau and Mouffe analysis would seem to imply.

The most important aspect of the Laclau/Mouffe analysis of hegemony is the attempt which they have made to move away from economistic, and politically oppressive, versions of communism, towards radical political issues. This entails reconstructing a socialist dimension to the fundamental values in radical liberal political philosophy: justice, equality, liberty, freedom of expression, peace, and the enjoyment of life. These were present in Marx originally, but became obscured by both some anti-humanist theoretical developments in structuralist Marxism, and the politically repressive developments in the Soviet Union and Eastern Europe, to such an extent that the very word 'socialism' in British English has begun to take on the same negative connotation for many people that it has had during much of this century in American English. A massive task of reconstruction is needed to make links between socialism as a form of political economy, and the values mentioned above of justice, liberty, peace, material well-being and equality, seem at all plausible. To many people the terms 'socialism' and freedom, justice, liberty, even equality, are almost opposites; the word 'socialism' connotes an oppressive state system, if not a police state, lack of personal freedoms, and a low standard of living compared with Western capitalist states. Many people living in the West perceive the situation in Eastern Europe as being one in which 'socialism' has come to seem to entail the lack of freedom of expression and a politically and culturally repressive atmosphere.

Kolakowski, for instance, in the context of a discussion of Asia and Africa, has claimed that: ' "socialism" sometimes means little more than that a country is ruled despotically and that no political opposition is allowed'.[13]

In seeking to counter such perceptions, Laclau and Mouffe argue that there is a need for major changes in the left's viewpoints, especially in its statism. For example they argue:

> statism — the idea that the expansion of the role of the state is the panacea for all problems; and economism (particularly in its technocratic version) — the idea that from a successful economic strategy there necessarily follows a continuity of political effects which can be clearly specified.[14]

The left, they argue, needs to grasp pluralism, to accept fully that there is no necessary connection between many of the new movements for change in the West and socialism, and that the workers do not constitute the 'universal class' which can liberate everyone else.[15] The new social movements which have grown up in the West in the last two or three decades, such as feminism, the Gay Movement, the Peace Movement, and those concerned with ecological issues, should be seen to possess their own specificity. They do not necessarily see themselves as being intrinsically connected with socialism. Indeed, socialism/communism is often seen as being as much of a problem as capitalism, and in some cases more so — as in the case of some of those groups and social movements concerned with environmental issues, nuclear weapons, and homosexuality for example. Nevertheless, Laclau and Mouffe still fail to grasp the depths of the problems involved in trying to communicate that socialism is necessary for further liberation and rationality in social and economic affairs. The say at one point:

> Of course, every project for radical democracy implies a socialist dimension, as it is necessary to put an end to capitalist relations of production, which are at the root of numerous relations of subordination; but socialism is one of the components of a project for radical democracy, not vice versa.[16]

But there is no 'of course' about it. Millions of people do not see the connection between democratic participation and socialism, partly as a result of statism, and partly as a result of the oppression in actually existing socialist societies throughout the world. To the contrary, the notion that it is advanced capitalism which safeguards political and cultural liberties in modern societies is widespread and deep-rooted in the West — and this with good reason, given the situation of protest movements in Eastern Europe and the Soviet Union.

Socialism, for Laclau and Mouffe, implies not only workers' self-management, for this could potentially exclude those concerned about other issues, ecological and environmental considerations for example. It means also participation by other groups in the 'social appropriation of production'.[17] This is an important point of connection with the major concerns which many people have to overcome statism in Western forms of socialism and in Eastern forms of communism. Democratic participation could be a growth point in the renewal of the meaning of socialism. However, it may well be necessary to cease using the word 'socialism' for some years, and to talk about 'radical democracy' instead, if the real issues are to be addressed by many people in Western societies.

In the Third World it is possible that the ideas and values of 'socialism' can still connote something positive to ordinary people, despite what Kolakowski has asserted. Something of this positive aspect of socialism is capable of being communicated to some groups in the West, such as those in voluntary organizations concerned with aid to the ill and starving in the world outside the affluent parts of capitalism, and in the churches. Kolakowski failed to mention the regimes of a non-socialist nature in Latin America, Africa, and parts of Asis, which are often brutal, lacking in freedom of expression, and tolerate no political opposition either. The politically autocratic, dictatorial regimes of both the left and right are found in conditions of economic underdevelopment, where a lack of any experience of political democracy combines easily, it seems all-too-often, with the role the military may play in such social formations.

In the West, however, there are a wide range of issues — unemployment, inflation, the sometimes huge discrepancies in incomes between managers and workers, poverty in old age, racialism, and Third World poverty and starvation — from which a start could be made to revitalize democratic socialism. The dimension of the Third World must be brought into the analysis too, for economic issues and matters of social justice are increasingly global in nature. Significant groups of people in the West, for instance, were offended by the food surpluses produced by Western agriculture when this was seen alongside the fact that people died of starvation in parts of Africa during the mid-nineteen-eighties. There is a large pool of untapped dissatisfaction with what are perceived as being the 'excesses' of capitalist materialism, especially the grosser forms of American capitalism, and the very rich capitalists to be found in other parts of the world, a dissatisfaction which can be found among many groups in Western Europe and even in the United states. Such groups are often to be found among those who might be called, broadly speaking, religiously motivated people. They do not appear in the mass media frequently, nor are they given much space in the capitalist press to present and discuss their views. But nevertheless they do exist.

ANTI-ESSENTIALISM

The concept of essence, once a major cornerstone of Western philosophy, has been criticized by existentialists and more recently by post-structuralists, including the recent work of E. Laclau and C. Mouffe (1985) discussed in the preceding section of this chapter. The concept of essence implies a claim that there are some characteristics — essential characteristics — which are possessed by certain objects such as social, economic formations, or by human beings, which exist independently of the discourses or theories which construct them. The criticisms turn on the claim that no such essences can be established outside of any discourse. It is language and its associated practices which construct 'essence', and it is therefore better to make this clear by avoiding any talk about an inner essence, such as human nature or even the essential characteristics of a mode of production.

There is a surprising similarity to be found between the criticism of the concept of essence in the work of some post-structuralists and the writings of an earlier generation such as those of Sartre — surprising because structuralism itself was seen as a reaction against the existentialism which had been dominant in French cultural life from the end of the Second World War to the late nineteen-fifties. Sartre once defined existentialism as the philosophy based upon the proposition that 'existence precedes essence'.[18] Post-structuralists can be seen as in part reviving the critique of essentialism which began with existentialists such as Sartre for they too hold that any 'essence' is a socio-lingusitic construction.

The terms 'essence' and 'existence' have been fundamental ones in European philosophy since the Middle Ages, but they have been given diverse meanings in different philosophical schemes. From man's essence being seen as the possession of a supernatural soul in Catholic philosophy, the essence of man came to be seen as his rational, thinking capacity, freed from dogma and external authorities, in the works of Descartes and Hume. The notion of essence went into moral/political decline in the early twentieth century when it became linked with politically reactionary views — in ideologies built up around the ideas of racial and national essences.[19]

The term 'essence' for Sartre connoted a conception of human nature which was given outside of existence. For example, the claim that a human infant could be born with certain desires already formed by its biology was denied and seen as a form of 'bad faith'. We are responsible for our choices and our desires, which are derived from the fundamental project a person chooses to make, Sartre argued. Desires and attitudes towards the world and other people do not exist, on this view, before a person has been socialized into a human culture. It was the essentialist conception of a given human nature which Sartre had aimed to combat in *Being and Nothingness*.

To imagine that anything was given at birth which could determine later choices was to be 'inauthentic' for Sartre. Authenticity lay in recognizing that man was free to choose; free to chose to do or be anything at all. One example Sartre gave was that of homosexuality. He argued that a homosexual was not determined to be a lover of the same gender by any determinations from his or her past, or from genetic constitution. Homosexual men and lesbian women had made a free choice of a fundamental project to develop their desires at some point in their lives, free from any determinations acting upon them. However, this seemed to be a mistaken view to many homosexual men and women themselves. Some felt that they were more determined in their sexual preferences than Sartre's position allowed for. Some wished to exercise a choice, to change to heterosexuality, but found in their own experience that they could not do so merely by willing it, nor by seeking to be changed through psychotherapy. Some psychotherapists themselves preferred the Freudian conception of the bisexual nature of the unconscious as an explanation of sexual desires of all kinds to the existentialist version of the unconscious developed by Sartre which seemed to miss, or deny, the experience of determination in the lives of many homosexuals.[20]

For Sartre human beings were not free to choose avoiding making a fundamental project of some kind in order to make the world meaningful. The world had no essential meaning that could be read off; the meaning of the world, of history, of an individual life, was a human construct. Consequently any form of Marxist economic determinism was rejected by Sartre, as was any notion of determination by the unconscious such as that found in Freudian psychoanalysis.

Marxism, when construed as a deterministic view of history, was 'inauthentic' for Sartre because it failed to allow for freedom of choice. Instead of basing its analysis of capitalism upon a satisfactory view of human existence as involving moral and political choice, orthodox, dogmatic Marxism had tried to impose a fixed system of meanings onto history. Sartre's existentialist Marxism was an attempt to find a philosophical base for socialism which would not produce the sterility and dogmatism of

Stalinism.[21] There was, moreover, no essence which made a person 'capitalist' or 'proletarian', anymore than there was an essence of Jew, or homosexual, for Sartrean existentialism. Nevertheless Sartre admitted that a particular person could have their freedom limited by the Other. For instance the ideology of anti-semitism, which reached its zenith as Sartre wrote, was a form of essentialist thinking which limited the freedom of those defined by others as Jews. Those affected could not alter the way they were defined by others simply by choosing, as an act of free consciousness, to ignore the actions taken against them.

Structuralism was an attempt to rectify some of the supposed shortcomings of Satrean existentialism among both some groups of Marxists, and some psychoanalysts such as Jacques Lacan, whilst preserving existentialism's rejection of essentialism, at least so it seemed. The notion of structures, however, rapidly came to seem like a new form of essence, and structuralism could be seen as a new form of essentialism. Although they were not seen as determinations, 'structures' were conceptualized as being outside human projects, outside human capacities to control. People were seen as being constructed by structures — economic, social, cultural and linguistic — but not as agents able to change these forms. This theoretical position was intended to mark a shift away from the humanism to be found in existentialism. In Althusser's work this approach led to a subtle form of determinism by structures outside of human agents' control or direction.

In the period since the dominance of structuralism, in what has come to be called post-structuralism, much has been made of trying to escape from essentialist thinking about politics in general, and about sexuality and gender in particular.[22] This has not entailed a full return to the problematic of Sartrean existentialism, but the same theme, the critique of the notion of essence, and of structures which came to play a role very similar to that of the notion of essence, is present. For instance, Laclau and Mouffe have written:

> The symbolic — i.e. overdetermined — character of social relations therefore implies that they lack an ultimate literality which would reduce them to necessary moments of an imminent law. There are not two planes, one of essence and the other of appearances, since there is not possibility of fixing an ultimate literal sense for which the symbolic would be a second and derived plane of signification. Society and social agents lack any essence . . . .[23]

In such an analysis as that of Laclau and Mouffe, there is no way of being able to assert anything meaningful about any essential needs and desires of human beings, for to do so would involve the presupposition that we have a language for describing what these are. There is no such language which is theory-neutral, independent of any discousre, such that these needs could be described and then tested to see if they can be established empirically. It follows, therefore, that no conceptions of human nature are possible, for this would be to re-introduce a conception of essence into social and political theory.

Until recently it has been assumed that Marxism rules out any possibility of an essentialist conception of human needs and desires. But does it? The view that it does has been based upon the sixth of Marx's *Theses on Feuerbach*:

> Feuerbach resolves the essence of religion into the essence of man. But the essence of man is no abstraction inherent in each single individual. In its reality it is the ensemble of the social relations.
>
> Feuerbach, who does not enter upon a criticism of this real essence, is hence obliged:
>
> 1. To abstract from the historial process and to define the religious sentiment by itself, and to presuppose an abstract — isolated — human individual.
> 2. Essence, therefore, can be regarded only as 'species', as an inner, mute, general character which unites the many individuals in a natural way.[24]

One recent writer, Norman Geras, has argued that there is no necessity to interpret this thesis as implying that Marx had no conception of human nature, that is, of the 'essence' of man. Geras discussed the possible interpretations of the claim made above that the essence of man 'is the ensemble of the social relations.' He concludes that Marx could be interpreted as meaning that:

> 1. In its reality the nature of man is conditioned by the ensemble of social relations.

Or:

> 2. In its reality human nature, or the nature of man, is manifested in the ensemble of social relations.

But not:

In its reality the nature of man is determined by, or human nature
is dissolved in, the ensemble of social relations.[25]

The argument turns on both this understanding of the sixth thesis and on
exegesis of Marx's other works. From the *German Ideology* for instance:

Men can be distinguished from animals by consciousness, by
religion or anything else you like. They themselves begin to
distinguish themselves from animals as soon as they begin to
produce their means of subsistence, a step which is conditioned by
their physical organization.[26]

In *Capital*, Volume 1, Marx speaks of 'the aggregate of those mental
and physical capabilities existing in the physical form, the living personality, of a human being', and 'the labour-power possessed in his bodily
organism by every ordinary man'.[27] The *Critique of the Gotha Programme* canvases 'the all-round development of the individual'.[28] There
is a view of the constitution of man operating in Marx, a view of man's
physical nature, which needs food, shelter, sunlight, recreation and work
activity, the latter leading to man's social relations, which are also needed
for the full realization of human potential.

This is important because any adequate moral and political phioosphy,
aiming to be hegemonic in the Gramscian sense, must be based upon some
conception of human nature, or human needs, in the light of which some
objectivity can be claimed for value judgements about specific sets of
political and economic arrangements. This is not mere moralizing, for these
values are linked to social relations, and a 'scientific' analysis, that is a
rational social theoretical position about what would have to change for the
values in question to be realized in a social formation. Furthermore, the
needs of men, women and children, are derived from a biological view of
man's nature — his physical requirements first, followed by a social-
psychological view about the social, economic and political arrangements
which would enable people to develop as creative human beings. The moral
and political position is dependent on a scientific view of man, not upon
speculation, nor upon religious authorities. Value judgements are related,
logically, to empirically based claims about human beings' physical and
biological needs and about their potentialities for creative development
beyond mere subsistence.

Without some view of human nature, containing both social and
biological propositions, it has been claimed that no 'scientific', or reasona-
bly universal and objective, basis for moral and political philosophy is
possible. A moral and political philosophy requires a view of human

nature, of the 'essence' of humanity where the notion of essence is understood as being about a set of needs and potentialities of the human species, so that this can form the basis for a political and social-economic theory which aims to realize the potential of human beings as far as possible, through the introduction of economic, social and political changes. Changes would be made which would enable human beings to be able to realize their potential as creative, loving, caring, social beings.[29]

This takes us a long way from Althusser's position of theoretical anti-humanism, and his preference for the later so-called scientific works of Marx rather than the Hegelian, humanistic writings. In my view, however, there is a need to redevelop the links between moral philosophy, social and political theory and practices, and to relate these to Marx's works as a whole, without trying to remove the humanism, or the transformed Hegalian concepts, or essentialist elements in them. Rather these have to be re-appropriated into social theory and moral philosophy if democratic socialism is to become a viable alternative in the West. This work is part of the meaning of a hegemonic project conceived of as moral, intellectual and philosophical leadership, or sense of direction, among the left in Britain, Western Europe, and not least in the United States.

This chapter has examined the work of Laclau and Mouffe which was anti-essentialist, but not thereby existentialist. The work of Sartre was discussed in the second section of this chapter to show the context in which first Althusser's anti-humanist intervention occurred, and post-structuralism emerged. The discussion by Geras of the idea that there is a conception of human nature in Marx was also mentioned. This latter viewpoint might be seen as echoing some of Gramsci's work, namely that the philosophy of praxis must be seen as including a coherent humanism, a view of human potentialities as well as basic needs. This conclusion leads in the opposite direction to that of the anti-humanism of Althusser, but it is one which can be seen as being more consistent with Gramsci's overall position than that of Althusser. The view that there is a theory of human nature, of essence in the sense of the potentiality of humanity, in Marx's work, and that this is an essential component of an adequate moral and political philosophy is one which also moves away from that of some post-Marxists. This does not mean that it is necessarily more 'correct', or more useful, for political or theoretical purposes. Only time will tell which of the developments discussed — the anti-humanism of Althusser, the anti-essentialist and 'post-Marxist' views of Laclau and Mouffe, or the humanist and more essentialist view of Geras, allied with Gramscian Marxism — is the most fruitful for developing a new moral and philosophical hegemony as a basis for political action to further the development of human potentialities in Western Europe and even in the United States.

REFERENCES

[1] E. Laclau & C. Mouffe, *Hegemony and Socialist Strategy. Towards a Radical Democratic Politics,* translated by W. Moore & P. Cammack, London, Verso Press, 1985.

[2] Ibid., p. 85.

[3] Ibid., p. 67.

[4] See N. Poulantzas, *Classes in Contemporary Capitalism,* London, New Left Books, 1975; A. Cutler, B. Hindess, P. Hirst, & A. Hussein, *Marx's Capital and Capitalism Today*, London, 1977; E. O. Wright, *Class, Crisis and the State,* London, New Left Books, 1978.

[5] See N. Poulantzas, op. cit. note in ref. [4] above.

[6] See K. Marx, *Wages, Price, and Profit*, Moscow, Foreign Languages Publishing House, first published 1898, pp. 94–95; and V. I. Lenin, *What is to be Done?* (1902), Moscow, Foreign Language Publishing House.

[7] E. Laclau & C. Mouffe, 1985, op. cit., pp. 95–96.

[8] Ibid., p. 113.

[9] Ibid., p. 113.

[10] Ibid., p. 112.

[11] F. Engels, *Socialism: Utopian and Scientific* (1892), Moscow, Foreign Languages Publishing House, p. 87.

[12] See F. Engels, Ibid., p. 55.

[13] L. Kolakowski, *Main Currents of Marxism,* vol. 3, 'The Breakdown', Oxford, Clarendon Press, 1978, p. 491.

[14] E. Laclau & C. Mouffe, 1985, op. cit., p. 177.

[15] Ibid., p. 167.

[16] Ibid., p. 178.

[17] Ibid., p. 178.

[18] J.-P. Sartre, *Existentialism is a Humanism*, New York, 1947.

[19] See H. Marcuse, 'On Essence', in *Negations. Essays in Critical Theory,* translated by J. Shapiro, Boston, Beacon Press, 1968, p. 44.

[20] See J.-P. Sartre, *Being and Nothingness*, translated by H. Barnes, London, Methuen, 1957, Part Four, Chapter Two, section I, 'Existential Psychoanalysis'.

[21] See J.-P. Sartre, *Critique of Dialectical Reason,* translanted by A. Sheridan-Smith, London, New Left Books, 1976.

[22] See J. Weeks, *Sex, Politics and Society*, London, Longman, 1981, chapter 1.

[23] E. Laclau & C. Mouffe, 1985, op. cit., p. 98.

[24] K. Marx, *Theses on Feuerbach* (1845), No. VI, as given in N. Geras, *Marx and Human Nature. Refutation of a Legend,* London, Verso

Press and New Left Books, 1983, p. 29. In each case I use N. Geras's quotations of Marx as they are the basis for his discussion. These differ from other translations, as in this case. The sixth thesis is given a slightly different translation, for example, in T. Bottomore and M. Rubel (eds.), *Karl Marx, Selected Writings in Sociology and Social Philosophy*, Harmondsworth, Pelican Books, 1971, pp. 83–84. Bottomore and Rubel use the term 'nature of man' where Geras uses 'essence'.

[25] N. Geras, op. cit. in ref. [24], p. 46.
[26] K. Marx, *German Ideology,* quoted by N. Geras, 1983, op. cit., pp. 66–67.
[27] Ibid., p. 82.
[28] Ibid., p. 85.
[29] See H. Marcuse, 'On Essence', in *Negations. Essays in Critical Theory* (first published 1936), op. cit. in ref. [19] above.

Conclusion

The major assumption underlying this book has been that the problematic of hegemony can enable social theory and sociology to move away from positivism in its various forms, all of which try to divorce moral and political philosophy from the 'social sciences'. The emphasis upon agency, upon consent and upon political will, in order to both understand and to achieve change, distinguish this approach from the theoretical 'anti-humanism' of structuralism and post-structuralism in which the role of human agency in social and political change appears to be lost. Such a social theory and associated sociology, centred upon the problematic of hegemony, can provide the basis, potentially at least, for the analysis of both modern capitalism and of actually existing socialisms.

One reason why such a social theory/sociology, however, cannot simply adopt Gramsci as a mentor, in spite of the foundational work he did in developing this new approach, is that he had only the Soviet Union, as a form of actually existing socialism, available to him from which to develop his analysis. However, the ideas he developed can be applied in the analysis of the more recently developed 'communist' regimes which have emerged since his time. There are now a number of actually existing socialist states around the world, in addition to the Soviet Union. Many people in the West assume that these socialist/communist social formations are not able to offer a way of life which the majority of people living in them desire. The fact that this assertion is untestable by questionaires and interviews, recognized as satisfactory by Western sociologists, serves to help substantiate this claim. The lack of freedom of expression in a social formation in which the dominant ideology is not hegemonic, that is, is rationally understood and has active consent given to it by a large number of people, generates suspicion, lack of openness and trust among people, and violence against opponents of the regime long after the revolutionary period is over. Communism can hardly be described as being 'hegemonic' in the areas of morality and philosophy, or in intellectual and cultural life more generally, through processes of active consent, rather than being 'dominant' as a result of the use of armed force, in all the countries of Eastern Europe, for example. Nevertheless, it should not be forgotten that the Soviet armed forces were fighting with the Western allies against Nazi Germany in the Second World War, and were seen in part as liberators from Nazi domination by many in the countries of Europe who had suffered from German invasion.

In other countries in the world, such as Cuba and China, we simply do not have enough knowledge upon which to form an adequate judgement about the degree of hegemonic consent 'communism' has in these societies. Both these countries' revolutions, however, appeared to have a high degree of initial popular support among large numbers of ordinary people at the beginning of their development which may well have continued to the present day. We in the capitalist West do not know in depth about the present situation regarding the nature of hegemonic leadership, as distinct from 'domination', in these social formations.

A further reason for not simply adopting Gramsci *in toto* as the foundation for social theory and sociology concerns the changes which have occurred in post-Second World War capitalism. Modern capitalism is in a stronger political and economic position in many social formations than it was in Gramsci's own lifetime, when fascism was emerging in Italy, Germany and elsewhere in Europe. This strength remains in spite of modern capitalism's recent problems with high levels of unemployment, which have not been as high, so far at least, as they were in the nineteen-twenties and -thirties. Modern capitalism's ideological strength remains high, however, in many parts of the world, including North America, Western Europe, Japan, New Zealand and Australia. This ideological approval derives, in part, from the material goods capitalism has provided for the majority of people in the West, and partly from the association which is made between capitalism and a high degree of cultural and political openness, tolerance and pluralism, compared with actually existing forms of socialism/communism.

Nevertheless, Gramsci's work on hegemony does provide a useful, indeed necessary, starting point for social theory which, in turn, could provide the basis for the more concrete analysis of a society such as modern Britain. A radical social theory in general, and a radical sociology in particular, would begin from the work of Marx and its extension in the work of later writers among whom Gramsci is of central importance. However, as was discussed in Chapter 4, Weber's work was developed also in the context of a critique of economistic, deterministic forms of Marxism and does, therefore, share some common themes with Gramsci. Weber's sociology of religion, together with the theme of the increasing rationalization of the modern world through bureaucratization and technology, remain useful and important starting points for modern social theory. A

Weberian dimension in sociology and social theory ensures that the crucial role of religions, and their value implications for social, economic, political, legal and cultural action in modern societies, is not overlooked or ignored.

There is in both Weber and in much American and British sociology, however, an avoidance of philosophy — philosophy in the sense of a coherent world-view as a basis for conducting sociology — which distinguishes it from the social theory and problematic of hegemony. The positivistically defined social sciences, sociology in particular, become logically incoherent in that they claim to be based upon a methodology which is 'scientific', in the sense of value-neutral and apolitical, yet cannot avoid making interpretative claims about social actions. These claims about social actions inevitably involve values which are implicit in the social scientists' language used to provide the interpretations of action. Such interpretative claims about social action have to be made within some theoretically informed language used by the interpreter. The decision to use one theoretical framework rather than another as a basis for interpretations involves values. One such core value concerns, for instance, the way in which human action itself is conceptualized as either being fully determined by outside forces, or as being potentially rational and free from determinations.

The users of statistical or quantitative languages cannot avoid the same type of problem in this respect as do qualitative interpretations of action, because value judgements are involved in the decision about which theory to use in order to quantify social actions, or speech acts, in the construction of the categories used to form tables of data. No theoretical language about human action, including those forming the basis from which the categories of analysis used in quantified tables of data are developed, is entirely free from ethical and political values. Statistical and mathematical 'languages' cannot avoid this central feature of any language used to describe, let alone account for, human actions. Quantification may serve the purpose of hiding the values of the researchers, the values, that is, which lie behind their choice of a theoretical framework of some kind, but it does not enable them to avoid the need to make such choices when they move from observations to the construction of categories for their tables of data.

Human actions are logically involved with values by virtue of being both 'human', as distinct from being purely physical, or biological, phenomena, and 'action' as distinct from causally determined behaviour patterns, or movements, of non-linguistic organisms. These features of human action cannot be wished away, or spirited away, by quantification. Inappropriate quantification applied to human actions mystifies the values held both by those being studied and by the researchers.[1]

Any sociology must be related to moral and political values if it is 'to make sense' to readers. Without being so related it appears free-floating and too often a pointless exercise to many people. The problem with values being introduced, from the outside as it were, into a social science, is that they appear to be arbitrary, the personal whim of the author, and can easily be rejected by someone who disagrees with that particular set of values. To counteract this kind of perception, the re-introduction of philosophical, rational, discussion of values and politics into social theory and the social sciences is necessary. This needs to be embedded within social theory rather than left outside the discourse. The advantage of the problematic of hegemony, from this point of view, is that it helps to focus attention upon which philosophy is hegemonic in a society, and upon the political and cultural processes involved in producing change in societies. Most importantly, it also involves paying explicit attention to the philosophy, or world-view, upon which the analysis is conducted, together with its associated moral and political values.

It should be borne in mind, however, that some societies may have no coherent philosophy which can be said to be hegemonic. This situation can arise either where the ruling group holds a world-view which is not held by the majority of the citizens of a state, or where there is a lack of agreement among the ruling group, or groups, themselves about any single philosophy being treated as the basic one. The first situation, in which a ruling group attempts to impose a world-view on others who do not consent to it, is often called 'totalitarian'. The second situation, where confusion reigns, is not properly described as 'pluralist' because this could be a relatively coherent world-view, but may be termed 'relativist'. In such a social situation people, including ruling groups, intellectuals, journalists, artists, and teachers, become confused, unable to work out an intellectually coherent, rational and moral point of view, or philosophy, and think that every world-view is as good as the next, that there is little to choose between them. In contrast to these situations, a society which has a hegemonic world-view is one in which a relatively coherent philosophy is shared by the ruling groups and by all major groups composing the society.

I have argued that the problematic of hegemony focuses attention particularly upon the moral and philosophical dimensions of a social formation. This theoretical perspective does not assume that major change in Western European and North American societies, for example, will arise necessarily in the economic sphere, as is assumed from within the econ-omic-corporate standpoint of economism, unionism and class-based politics. An example of a non-economic phenomenon is to be found in the area which Gramsci termed 'the national-popular'. In Britain this centrally involves the civic rituals and values surrounding the Royal family, for instance. Religion, the mass media and the arts, ethnicity and race, science and technology, gender and sexuality, all these areas are significant zones of stability, or potential change, in modern social formations, which require analysis and incorporation into a wider political and social theory. This approach does not replace the economic dimension but adds to it. However, it does challenge economic determinism. In this sense it was said that Gramsci can be called the Weber of Marxism.

However, for Gramsci a social theory which makes the concept of hegemony central must be based upon a radical political philosophical position. This marks a difference with Weber's position of value-neutrality in the carrying out of sociological analysis, but Weber did hold that sociology must be conducted upon the basis of 'value-relevance', that is from some political and moral perspective which underpins any social scientific analysis. (Weber's own value position was that of an early twentieth-century German 'liberal'.)

A radical political philosophy is based upon the central values of rationality as the basis for authority, of freedom of thought and expression, of justice and equality. Radicalism, in this sense, contrasts with conservative philosophical emphases upon authority, allegiance and tradition.[2] This kind of conservatism would freeze any set of existing inequalities and injustices by maintaining the all-important values of allegiance to authority and tradition.

Radical political philosophy cannot be imposed by force, by means of a coercive state apparatus, because to be radical means to be rational in social, economic, political, and cultural matters. Rationality cannot be imposed upon people either by force or by traditional religious authorities. By definition, to conduct social, economic, political affairs on the basis of rational criteria, which is what carrying out radical political policies would entail, can only be done by gaining people's consent, not by forcing them to be free. For a radical philosophy, or world-outlook, to seek to be 'hegemonic' means that it must aim to win through rational understanding, together with emotional and moral consent among large and varied groups of people; it cannot be imposed, therefore, by force. A view similar to this was discussed in Chapter 5 in relation to the recent work of E. Laclau and C. Mouffe. Their position, however, emphasizes the lack of connections between the different aspects of a social formation — the economy, money, law, politics, education and religion — more than the view I took in that chapter or take here.

The term 'rational' as I use it above does not entail being scientific in a narrow or dogmatic sense. Scientism has dogged both Western positivist social sciences and Marxism, especially in its official forms as the state ideology in the Soviet Union and Eastern Europe. Marxism has been presented sometimes as the true science of history, that is, as having discovered the scientific laws governing the development and inevitable collapse of capitalism. This position has been used to justify bureaucratic centralism. Such developments have turned Marxism–Leninism into an ideology for a new elite of rulers to govern if needs be against the wishes of many of the ordinary citizens. Those who know the secrets of the science of history think that they, therefore, have a right to rule without necessarily gaining the consent of major groups in the society.

Turning to the situation in modern Britain, it is interesting to look at some recent social and political developments in the light of the social theory which takes the concept of hegemony as central in the analysis of a society or social formation. An important point to remember is that Marxism, considered as a political and moral philosophy, has not been strong in British political parties on the left in the past. The majority of social democratic and democratic socialist politicians have claimed that the values they espouse are derived either from a religious tradition, as in the case of Christian Socialism, or from the broadly based values of parliamentary democracy, or both. British social democracy and democratic socialism developed from Christianity. These political movements have produced the post-World War Two welfare state, the state taking over from the churches in the provision of education and medical care. Low levels of unemployment were maintained until the end of the nineteen-seventies, not only in Britain but throughout the developed industrial countries of capitalism. During the first half of the nineteen-eighties, however, unemployment in Britain reached levels not seen since the nineteen-twenties and -thirties. British levels of unemployment were significantly higher than in other similar Western industrial societies.[3] Yet this situation did not produce a victory for the Labour Party in the 1983 General Election. In spite of high unemployment, the Conservatives won a second term in government in 1983 — something which would once have been thought to be virtually impossible by many in the Labour Party and trades union movement who operate with economistic assumptions. These groups failed to grasp the importance of a wider moral philosophical campaign.

The lack of a rationally articulated, radical philosophical viewpoint in British political life, however, might be said to have reached its zenith in recent times when the majority of members of the House of Commons supported the Falklands/Malvinas War in 1982. Many speakers in the debate about the sending of the task force to expel the Argentinians from the islands assumed that there was a direct parallel with the war against Nazi Germany in 1939. Neither the Conservatives, nor most Labour politicians, nor Liberals, nor Social Democrats, had any response to Argentina's invasion of the Falkland/Malvinas Islands than to support the war, which led to the killing of 256 British combatants, 3 Falklanders, and at least 1,800 Argentinians. More people were killed in the war than the total population living on the islands.[4] A small number of politicians did voice their reservations about the war at the time, arguing for the involvement of the United Nations, but they were not heard amidst the furore of British patriotism generated by the episode.

The British 'victory' in the Falkalnds/Malvinas war is held by some to have contributed to the Conservatives winning the 1983 General Election. No doubt it did, but it must be remembered too that President Reagan was re-elected in the United States in 1985; the right also won elections in West Germany, in France and in Japan in 1986. Capitalism was popular enough in all the major industrial countries, including Britain, to allow what might be called the 'New Right' in the sense of the monetarist right, to win elections in the early and mid-nineteen-eighties.

The specific problems facing Britain have to be understood in the wider context of international capitalism, especially that of the United States and Western Europe. Britain shares a common language with the United States, a related popular culture in music, film and television, and similar sources for its political philosophy and jurisprudence in the work of Hobbes, Locke and Mill.[5] It is also closely involved militarily with Washington, being increasingly dependent upon the United States for nuclear weapons systems.

Industrially and commercially Britain has become more and more involved with Western Europe, its largest trading partner during the early nineteen-eighties being West Germany. Yet the integration of Britain with the European Economic Community has not been an easy process, and there are still tensions and differences of outlook whichever party is in power in Britain. Under both Labour and Conservative governments Britain remained an off-shore partner during the first decade of membership, having joined in 1974. British politicians still try to avoid the development of a common European currency and have held out against a common postage stamp in Europe on the grounds that the post in Britain must carry the monarch's head on the stamp! The fear of creeping European federalism runs very deep among most British politicians.

Britain remains caught, therefore, between the two worlds of Western Europe and the United States. Neither of these two larger economic and political units has been able, so far, to assert full political, economic, military, cultural, moral and philosophical hegemonic leadership over the British state, economy and civil society. Equally, however, Britain cannot assert its own hegemonic moral and philosophical leadership, as it was once able to do, upon the world stage. This is partly as a consequence of the loss of economic power over the decades since the nineteen-fifties, in comparison with the countries of Western Europe, especially West Germany and

France, and with Japan. The United States had taken over the role of dominant world economic and financial power from Britain, in any case, effectively at the end of the First World War.[6]

The loss of hegemonic leadership by Britain in the economic, moral and political spheres in those parts of the world once under British rule, or influence, has begun to have important internal effects within the society itself. Without her colonies Britain appears to be a relatively small country, no longer the centre of a large empire. In this changed situation, which became effectively finalized in the nineteen-sixties, no one political party, or alliance of parties, has been able to lead hegemonically in modern Britain. During the period of de-colonization all the major parties agreed upon the moral and political desirability of that process. Since it ended no comparable moral and political task has unified the parties in external affairs. There has been too much ambivalence about the European Community for this to have become the significant international venture it could have been. Increased economic, political and cultural integration with Europe, however, remains the only realistic option for Britain's future, but there is a strange failure on the part of British politicians to grasp the full implications of this and to lead people towards it. On matters connected with the internal economy, no successful policy has been found which can halt Britain's relative decline in terms of the material standard of living of the population when compared with other advanced industrial countries. No one political economic philosophy can claim success; consequently no one economic set of policies is able to command support among all social and economic groups.

This contrasts with the situation in the United States where President Reagan became a national figure in his second term as President during 1985 and 1986. It has not been the personality of President Reagan which alone was able to exert hegemonic leadership, although he was an important and effective figurehead. Rather it has been the case that capitalistic commercial values, including a private profit-making orientation even among doctors for example, are held to be legitimate ones to apply to most spheres of life by many major groups among the population in the United States. In Britain, on the other hand, non-commercial values do hold some legitimacy, in the eyes of most major groups, especially in certain spheres including medicine, social work and education. This partly reflects Britain's feudal legacy and the absence of such a feudal past in the United States, but it reflects too the general acceptance of the Welfare State among most of the major groups in Britain outside of the capitalist entrepreneurial and managerial classes. In this situation it cannot be said that British capitalism is hegemonic in the way it is in the United States.

In the same period of the mid-nineteen-eighties, when President Reagan enjoyed majority support, Mrs Thatcher's position appeared vulnerable in electoral terms, but more importantly, in the context of the problematic of hegemony, she had lost the capacity to lead in moral and philosophical terms — even if it is supposed that 'Thatcherism' was ever really hegemonic. No other political party, leader or group in Britain has managed to establish hegemonic leadership either. This, to reiterate, is not the same thing as winning an election because to exercise moral and intellectual leadership hegemonically involves a more widespread and deeper-rooted process than gaining a majority of votes, or rather seats in the legislature. In this sense the pop singer, Bob Geldof, who organized the movements of both pop stars and sports persons to raise money for famine relief and aid to Africa in 1985 and 1986, had more right to be considered as a moral leader, expressing and articulating a moral perspective held by millions of all age groups in Britain and elsewhere in the industrial world, than the political leaders and parties.[7]

However, it cannot be said that these movements represented a form of intellectual or philosophical leadership. Concentrating as they did on pop music and sport, these movements represented the anti-intellectualism which modern forms of capitalism encourage, especially in the mass media. No new hegemonic philosophy can be produced without challenging, rather than reinforcing, the anti-intellectual and a-philosophical mass culture. It was, nevertheless, a most important moral and political event.

Morally a significant vein was tapped by Band Aid, Live Aid and Sport Aid among millions of people. Intellectually, in terms of political philosophy, however, the movements hardly scratched the surface. Some teachers and clergy have used the events as a way of teaching something about international economics and finances, about the organization of agriculture in Europe, the United States, in Africa, Latin America and in communist systems. The mainstream politicians were irrelevant to either the organization of the events, or to the educational process of follow-up they required. Band Aid, Live Aid and Sport Aid were nevertheless important examples of a limited form of moral, hegemonic leadership being exercised in civil society.

The problematic which has the concept of hegemony at its centre remains of vital importance not only for the empirical analysis of modern societies, but also for the renewal of a coherent, and relevant, political and social theory, based upon a rational, radical, moral and political philosophy. Moral and political philosophy cannot be made to disappear from the disciplines of politics, sociology, economics or history in the way positivists and relativists in various guises have attempted to do. The Gramscian concept of hegemony reminds us that this is so, and provides a foundation for renewing social theory.

REFERENCES

[1] Gramsci wrote on the theme of the underlying political and ethical issues involved in statistics, as in the following passage: 'the fact has not been properly emphasised that statistical laws can be employed in the science and art of politics only so long as the great masses of the population remain (or at least are reputed to remain) essentially passive . . . Indeed in politics the assumption of the law of statistics as an essential law operating of necessity is not only a scientific error, but becomes a practical error in action'. (A. Gramsci, Selections from the *Prison Notebooks*, edited and translated by Q. Hoare & G. Nowell-Smith, London, Lawrence & Wishart, 1971.

[2] See R. Scruton, *The Meaning of Conservatism*, Harmondsworth, Penguin, 1980.

[3] The United Kingdom had 11.9% unemployed in 1984. This was higher than both France (10.2%) and West Germany (8.4%). Italy was the same as the UK (11.9%). Holland was higher (14.4%) as was Belgium (14.4%). Spain had 20.6%, the highest in Europe. Portugal's rate (10.7%) was lower than that of the UK. Sources: EEC and OECD.

[4] See A. Barnett, *Iron Britannia. Why Parliament Waged its Falklands War*, London, Allison & Busby, 1982, pp. 15 and 21.

[5] See the work of the American political philosopher John Rawls, *A Theory of Justice*, Oxford, Oxford University Press, 1972 and 1978.

[6] For example, R. Dahrendorf, *On Britain*, London, British Broadcasting Corporation, 1982. See especially Chapters 2, 3, 4, 5, 17, 18, 19, 20, 21, 22, and 23. These chapters are all relatively short ones!

[7] See S. Hall & M. Jacques, 'People Aid: a new politics sweeps the land', in *Marxism Today*, London, July 1986, pp. 10–14.

Further Reading

These suggestions for further reading include: first the major texts which are relevant to the development of the concept of hegemony; second the texts in which the foundations of the concept of hegemony are to be found; finally the more recent texts in which the concept of hegemony is critically discussed or developed.

(1) EARLY TEXTS RELEVANT TO THE CONCEPT OF HEGEMONY

In the work of Marx there is no direct mention of the notion of hegemony. The main texts of Marx which are particularly relevant to the later development of the idea of hegemony are:

K. Marx, *The Class-Struggles in France (1848–50)*, first published 1850, reprinted in 1895 with a preface by F. Engels. Available in *Surveys from Exile. Political Writings,* Vol. 2, edited and introduced by D. Fernbach, The Pelican Marx Library, Harmondsworth, Penguin Books Ltd, in association with *New Left Review,* 1973.

K. Marx, *The Eighteenth Brumaire of Louis Bonaparte*, first published in 1852, translated by D. de Leon, 1898. Available in *Surveys from Exile,* Vol. 2, see above.

K. Marx, *The Civil War in France*, first published in 1871 in English.

K. Marx, *Critique of the Gotha Programme*, first published in 1875.

V. I. Lenin, *What is to be Done?*, first published 1902, Moscow, Foreign Language Publishing House.

V. I. Lenin, *The State and Revolution*, first published 1917, 2nd edn 1918, Moscow, Foreign Languages Publishing House.

Also relevant:

B. Croce, *History as the Story of Liberty*, London, Allen & Unwin, 1941, p. 33–34; first published in Italian as *La Storia come Pensiero e come Azione*, 1938.

(2) GRAMSCI'S INTERVENTION:

The recent discussion about hegemony stems from renewed interest in the work of Antonio Gramsci. Gramsci's main works which are available in English are:

A. Gramsci, *Selections from the Prison Notebooks of Antonio Gramsci,* edited and translated by Q. Hoare & G. Nowell Smith, London, Lawrence & Wishart, 1971. This is a selection from the original Italian edition: A. Gramsci, *Quaderni del Carcere* (1928–1935), six volumes, edited by V. Gerratana, Turin, Einaudi, 1948–51.

A. Gramsci, *Selections from Political Writings, 1910–1920*, selected and edited by Q. Hoare, translated by J. Mathews, London, Lawrence & Wishart, 1977.

A. Gramsci, *Selections from Political Writings, 1921–1926*, edited and translated by Q. Hoare, London, Lawrence & Wishart, 1978.

(3) LATER DEVELOPMENTS OF THE NOTION OF HEGEMONY

The major discussions either of the Gramscian concept of hegemony explicitly, or related to it more implicitly, which are relevant to the discussion in this book, include the following:

L. Althusser, *For Marx*, London, Allen Lane, 1969.

L. Althusser, *Lenin and Philosophy and Other Essays*, London, Verso Press, 1977.

P. Anderson, 'The Antinomies of Antonio Gramsci', in *New Left Review,* No. 100, 1976–77, London, pp. 5–78.

C. Buci-Glucksmann, *Gramsci and the State*, translated by D. Fernbach, London, Lawrence & Wishart, 1980.

J. Femia, *Gramsci's Political Thought. Hegemony, Consciousness and Revolutionary Process,* Oxford, clarendon Press, 1981.

N. Geras, *Marx and Human Nature. Refutation of a Legend,* London, Verso Press and New Left Books, 1983.

S. Hall, 'The "political" and the "Economic" in Marx's Theory of Classes', in A. Hunt (ed.), *Class and Class Structure*, London, Lawrence & Wishart, 1978, pp. 19–35. Reprinted in R. Bocock *et al., An Introduction to Sociology*, London, Fontana, 1980, pp. 197–237.

E. Laclau & C. Mouffe, *Hegemony and Socialist Strategy. Towards a Radical Democratic Politics,* translated by W. Moore & P. Cammack, London, Verso Press, 1985.

H. Marcuse, *Negations. Essays in Critical Theory*, translations from the

German by J. Shapiro, Boston, Beacon Press, 1968. See chapter 2, 'The Concept of Essence'.

A. Showstack Sassoon (ed.), *Approaches to Gramsci*, London, Writers and Readers, 1982, 'Passive Revolution and the Politics of Reform'.

R. Simon, *Gramsci's Political Thought. An Introduction,* London, Lawrence & Wishart, 1982.

P. Worsley, *Marx and Marxism*, Chichester and London, Ellis Horwood and Tavistock Publications Limited, 1982.

Index